THE SIMPLE GUIDE TO

ISLAM

ABOUT THE AUTHOR

DANIELLE ROBINSON was born and bred in the South of France (Toulouse). In 1971 she married Neal Robinson, today a leading authority in Islamic Studies and author of *The Sayings of Muhammad*, London 1991. Subsequently, Danielle taught French throughout England and now lives in Yorkshire where she is an Honorary Visiting Fellow at the University of Bradford. She is currently closely involved in Cultural studies relating to Islam in France, and in particular the representation of Muslim women.

For Khadijah & Nudrat – our Bradford friends

Ewar – symbol of purification

DRAWINGS BY
IRENE SANDERSON

THE SIMPLE GUIDE TO

ISLAM

Danielle Robinson

GLOBAL BOOKS LTD

Simple Guides ● Series 3
WORLD RELIGIONS

The Simple Guide to
ISLAM
By Danielle Robinson

First published 1997 by
GLOBAL BOOKS LTD
PO Box 219, Folkestone, Kent, England CT20 3LZ

ⓒ 1997 Global Books Limited

Reprinted 1999, 2001

ISBN 1-86034-013-X

British Library Cataloguing in Publication Data
A CIP catalogue entry for this book
is available from the British Library

Set in Futura 10½ on 11½ point by Bookman, Slough
Printed in Great Britain by The Cromwell Press, Wiltshire

Contents

*   *   *

List of Illustrations

Preface

IT is a great privilege for a scholar to be immersed in a subject which fascinates him and to feel that he is helping to roll back the frontiers of knowledge. Nevertheless, the bestowal of privileges usually imposes duties. I have long believed that scholars in universities have a duty to write simple books for the larger public who have neither the time nor the inclination to wade through hundreds of pages of academic prose. Thus when Paul Norbury asked me to write *The Simple Guide to Islam*, I accepted the invitation despite realizing that it might prove difficult to fit the work in with all my other duties as a teacher, researcher and administrator.

After several months spent drafting chapters at weekends, it became clear that the book I was writing was not the one that I had been asked to write. It was relatively simple and relatively brief but it was going nonetheless to be some three or four times the required length. At this point Danielle, my life partner, saved the day by offering to share the task. She is not a specialist in Islamic Studies, at least not in the conventional sense. Over the past twenty years, however, she has read many books and articles on the subject including everything that I have written. She has accompanied me on numerous trips to Morocco, Tunisia and Syria; she had all 1250 pages of Doughty's *Travels In Arabia Deserta* read to her in lieu of bedtime stories; and she spent much of her time living and working amongst Muslims in Bradford. More than this, she has a sharp mind and asks the kind of awkward question that the intelligent lay person might be expected to ask.

At first, we thought of joint authorship; but now that I have read the book through I feel that it is Danielle's creation. I provided the raw ingredients from which she selected what she needed. She added the sauce without which it would be nowhere near as palatable. Of course, there are a few places where I would not have put things quite as she has, but there are many more where I could not have done, try as I might!

Neal Robinson
THE UNIVERSITY OF LEEDS
August 1997

Introduction

Sixteenth-century velvet brocade used by the Ottoman Sultan

WE ONCE experienced a culture shock. The fact that its waves still affect us twenty years later must be proof of its impact. It was a benign enough occasion: a young Franco-English couple had crossed the Mediterranean for the first time for a winter holiday in Tunisia with their baby daughter. From an England where trains were delayed because of snow and ice, they were transported into a mild climate matched by the kindness of its people to children and foreigners.

On the local train taking them from Tunis, via Carthage, to Sidi Bou Said, they fell into conversation with an urbane, educated, bilingual Tunisian, who was willing to discuss any topic, including religion. They were shocked to discover that he thought that Christians worshipped three gods! How could such a perception of Christianity, whose members would all defend the unity of God, have arisen? And if such a well-meaning Muslim could hold such bizarre views, what was it like on the Christian side? What dreadful misrepresentations might Christians carry with them of Islam without even knowing it?

Neal returned from the holiday committed to learning Arabic so that he could read the Quran and Muslim theology, in the original. This he achieved and has since become a highly regarded Arabist. As for myself, via Cultural Studies in French, I have pursued the thread in a different way, for example, monitoring the clashes in French society when they centre on Muslims or children of Muslim immigrants. I read their books and books about them, I watch their films and films about them, as well as media reports.

In one of their books, entitled *Georgette*, the clash of commitments is such that the Muslim pupil who is pushed to learn to read and write in French by her non French-speaking father, must follow his advice. Every night, she has to copy out her homework starting from the back of the book and writing from right to left. On the first line, in order to bless her work, her father has even laboriously traced the Arabic for *Bismillah*, 'In the name of God'. Every morning, however, the teacher opens the girl's exercise-book at the front and punishes her for the unexplained blank page. As the girl lies dying under the wheels of a car, trying to flee the nightmarish situation, she feels as if she were gasping for air at the 'bottom of an ink-well'. It is only a novel, of course, but it is good to know that by reading books about others people are trying to understand one another.

And so it is that you are reading this book. And so it is that I have taken the opportunity offered by gentle goading from the publisher to write it, relying on full access to Neal's on-going work and library to put together some reflexions on 'basic' Islam. They are not meant to be exhaustive but to provide an informed basis for readers who, like me, have often pondered.

In the meantime, Neal is finishing a much meatier and informative volume with the working title of 'Islam, a Concise Introduction'. He is also planning a round of visits to France for his next book which will be on French Muslims. People have no idea how much 'pillow-talk' is devoted to Muslim matters! A case of a 'pas-de-deux' perhaps?

Danielle Robinson
UNIVERSITY OF BRADFORD
August 1997

Ottoman architecture – mosque of Sultan Ahmed, Istanbul, 1609-16

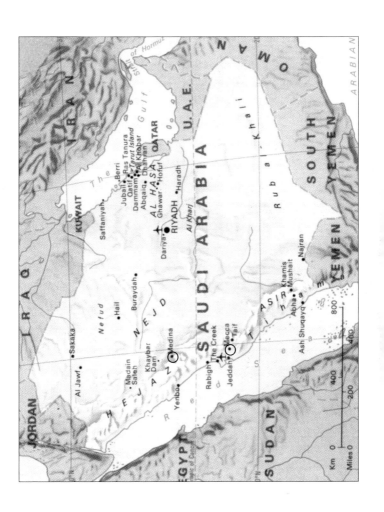

15

1 Muhammad, the Messenger of God

Evening prayer at the Great Mosque, Damascus

Aلthough the spelling 'Muhammad' is now acknowledged to be the most accurate English rendering of the Arabic pronunciation, people have hesitated between other forms like Moham(m)ed, Mohamet, Mahomet, which in turn have produced a crop of adjectives as in 'the Mohamedan religion', at different stages of Western writing on Islam.

The name of the founder of Islam is often followed by 'p.b.u.h.', which are the initials of the words of benediction uttered by believers as they use his name. They stand for '**p**eace and **b**lessings be **u**pon **h**im', a translation of the Arabic words meant to represent the reverence which accompanies thinking about Muhammad and makes one physically stop and ponder on the divine compassion in the middle of one's earthly pursuits.

'For the occidental reader there are grave difficulties in attaining a balanced understanding of the historical role of Muhammad.' Thus warned by W. Montgomery Watt, one of the world's specialists, in his chapter on Muhammad in the *Cambridge History of Islam*, we must tread carefully. He lists three reasons for our difficulty:

Our usual expectation of the separation between the private, religious domain, and public affairs is one reason, whereas Muhammad the religious leader 'was responding not merely to what the occidental would call the religious and intellectual aspects of the situation, but also the economic, social and political pressures to which Mecca was subject'. W. Montgomery Watt's second point is that the bitterness of encounters on the battlefields from the Middle-Ages onwards has meant that more negative propaganda than informed opinion has been passed on to us. His third point concerns the more dispassionate reality of distinguishing facts from legends among documents of such an early period. All other quotations in this chapter are from this work.

Painting from Siyar-i-Nabi (*Life of the Prophet*), 1594

The 'Revelations' & Rivalries

At the age of about forty, around the year 610, in Mecca in Arabia, Muhammad started talking about 'revelations' he was having from a 'messenger' of God commissioning him as a 'messenger of God' to the Arab people. The different ways in which these occurred do not matter here, but he was quite clear that they were not of his own making and 'whether the messages came from Muhammad's unconscious, or the collective unconscious functioning in him, or from some divine source, is beyond the competence of the historian'.

The external politics of his city were based on the neutrality it needed to maintain between the two world powers of that time, the Persian empire – officially Zoroastrian and tolerant towards Judaism – on the one hand, and the Christian Byzantine empire on the other, since Mecca's trade routes placed it in the middle of the clash. Internally, although one tribe, the Quraysh, lived there, the clan divisions were strong and the great wealth which had been obtained in Mecca due to its control of the caravan trade had not benefited them all. Rather it had accrued to some rich merchants who no longer honoured the old attitudes prevalent in the previous nomadic economy where possessions were the clan's rather than the individual's.

Muhammad was a posthumous child, who according to Arab custom was disqualified from his father's property. He worked in the caravan trade in a subordinate position until his marriage at twenty-five to Khadija, a rich older woman who had been impressed by his ability and honesty. Very little is known of his life until he began sharing his revelations, first with her, then with a growing group of friends and foes. Their only child to survive infancy into full adulthood was their daughter Fatima, who was beloved of her father and married Ali, his cousin. Together with the Prophet's grandsons, Hasan and Hussein, they are important in the development of Islamic history and doctrine. It is worth noting that neither Muhammad nor Ali married other women while their first wives were alive.

Muhammad Emigrates to Medina

The rich merchants tried to stop Muhammad from preaching his message which they feared would interfere with their supremacy built on the pursuit of riches. Offers of a place among them or pressure on his clan (the Hashim) to stop protecting him, failed to affect him until the head of the clan, his uncle, died in 619. He was also saddened by the death of his faithful wife and comforter, Khadija. Life became very difficult for him and his followers but proposals started coming from citizens of another city, Medina, asking him to settle there as their arbiter in internal clan disputes. In 622, he emigrated to Medina with his followers; this key date is known as the *hijra* and marks for Muslims the beginning of the Islamic era, that is to say Year 1 of the Islamic calendar.

Muhammad's power increased in Medina and he was able to conduct attacks on caravans from Mecca in the usual *razzia* (raid) tradition of show of strength and taking of booty with little loss of life, building his reputation and attracting more followers. Two notable events must be recorded for the year 624. One is religious and symbolizes the break from the Jews: as Muhammad was leading the prayers facing Jerusalem in the usual way, a revelation came that from now onwards, worshippers were to face Mecca as their *qibla* (direction of prayer) indicating that Islam was to develop as a separate religion, the religion of Abraham restored to its purity. The second event is politico-military: so far, the razzias had been conducted by the Muslim immigrants from Mecca (*Muhajirun*) who had found refuge in Medina. Now, Medinan Muslim converts (*Ansar*) offered to join in and a group consisting of about 300 men went to ambush a Meccan caravan. Although the caravan, which had been warned, eluded them, a party of 900 Meccans decided to punish their attempt and a fight took place at the Badr wells which was a great victory for Muhammad's group.

The Meccans were shocked by his growing success which challenged their supremacy. They attacked Medina in 625 at the site of Uhud, and although the Meccans withdrew indecisively, loss of life among the Muslims prompted much heart-searching. In order to provide for the widows of the men fallen at Uhud, Muslims were encouraged to take up to four wives, (a practice which did not go against monogamy, which was not an established norm, but rather against the matrilineal kinship which prevailed in some clans). Muhammad was aware of the Meccans' intention to destroy him and was ready for them when they set siege to Medina in 627 with enormous forces. They failed.

Power & Reconciliation

As a religious leader, Muhammad was urging people throughout Arabia to acknowledge God; as he now also wielded great political power, he could guess that many more followers were being attracted to him, even from Mecca. To this end he pursued a policy of reconciliation and overtures. Part of his successful negotiations occurred through his and his family's marriages into former enemy clans, whether pagan or Jewish, or neighbours, now eager for alliance. The ruler of Egypt for instance sent two slave-girls, one of whom he kept as a concubine rather than a wife, since as a Copt she preferred to remain a Christian. There was great joy when she gave him a son but distress when the boy died soon after birth. When a party of his early Meccan followers who had fled to the protection of Abyssinia, returned to his now established community in Medina, they were incorporated and feted with shares of booty they had not yet earned. Muhammad also married a Muslim widow returnee who was the daughter of Abu Sufyan, one of his main opponents in Mecca. Other women asked him to marry them at different stages of his life.

In 630 at the height of his success, when proud Mecca surrendered to him peacefully thanks to his father-in-law's mediation, and he had become the most powerful leader in the peninsula, he developed the concept of *jihad* or holy war, no longer as a razzia against one's neighbours since most of them were fast becoming part of the Muslim community, but against non-Muslims further afield. The war had to stop with no advantage won if these people became Muslims. This was a brilliant method of uniting men, brought up on the local 'sport' of raiding, into a disciplined army ready to carry out the formidable advances of Islam which were about to ensue, as the Persian empire was unbelievably about to collapse and Byzantium had reached an exhausted stage.

Purging Paganism

At the same time as Muhammad was highly successful in removing paganism (he purged the Kaaba of idols, Ch.6) and organizing a thriving community for which he was still receiving revelations, he experienced sadness and tensions at home as more of his daughters and grandchildren died and his wives quarrelled. He decided to offer them the choice of being divorced and therefore free to remarry or to carry on with the existing arrangements in a better spirit. One of them was Ayesha (Aisha), the only virgin he had married and she was the young daughter of his chief supporter, Abu Bakr who himself became Caliph after Muhammad's death (Ch.2). Ayesha and eight others decided to continue and were given positions of honour in the community as 'mothers of the believers', with the understanding that they would not wish to remarry after his death. Ayesha was the one to whose apartment he retired in June 632, after asking permission from his other wives to forego his customary conjugal rota. He died a few days later.

W. Montgomery Watts concludes: 'All in all, the rapid Arab expansion, with the ensuing spread of Islam and growth of Islamic culture, was the outcome of a complex of historical factors; but the set of ideas and the body of men capable of giving a unified direction to the expansion would not have existed but for the unique combination of gifts in Muhammad himself.'

Muhammad the Prophet & Messenger

This outline of the life of Muhammad does not deal with the content of his revelations, which gave its

Umayyad mosque in Cordoba, founded by Abd al-Rahman I,
785AD

driving force to Islam. Muhammad himself did not write any of these revelations but the community of faith memorized them carefully. How the **Quran** took its written form is explained in the chapter 4 on the 'Holy Text'. Muhammad was and is loved and revered, but never worshipped, since the centrality of his message is the oneness of God. He claimed to be a Prophet, the last in the long line of 'prophets', beginning with Adam, who were sent by God to turn human hearts to worship Him. Some of them, far fewer in number, were also 'messengers' to whom God revealed his law. Muhammad was one of their lineage which includes Abraham, Moses, and Jesus. He was sent to the Arabs, who had once been privileged to learn from Abraham but had subsequently lapsed to the pagan state of affairs prevalent in Mecca. There were some Christians in the Arabian peninsula and some were met in lands visited by the Meccan traders; they were mainly known as the political power of the Byzantine empire. Muhammad saw his message as a renewal offered by God to them as they had received the original message of Jesus, but had corrupted it over the years.

As for the Jews, complex policies are associated with the 'break with the Jews', who made up about a third of the Medinan population. The religious watershed of the change of *qibla* has been mentioned. The political and military oppositional stages extend from his arrival in Medina to the aftermath of the Meccan siege of the city. Muhammad had first hoped to collaborate with them since they had benefited from prophetic revelations before. He was then bitterly disappointed when they opposed him and their clans sided with rival Medinan leaders, especially when they covertly cooperated with

Meccan attackers during the battle of Uhud and again during the siege of Medina. A first clan was expelled after Badr, a second after Uhud and their remaining strongholds were destroyed after the siege of Medina.

Islam – the Purified 'Religion of Abraham'

The formulation of Islam as the purified 'religion of Abraham' specific to the Arabs and centred on Mecca whilst acknowledging its links with Christianity and Judaism, was forged in those early years. In conquered territories, Jews and Christians who decided to keep their religion were protected as 'people of the book'. Certainly, they were subjected to tax, and could not serve in the army, but there was no pressure to convert and their persons and property were safe, more than could be said of the situation of Jews in medieval Europe, or of the Muslims residing in Palestine when the Crusaders were the rulers.

Chapter 4 on 'Holy text' will cover the origins of Muslim beliefs and religious practices. But first a chapter on Islamic history which attempts to take the reader from the death of Muhammad in 632 to the present day.

2 Islamic History

Battle between Tamujin and the Emir of Cathay from a
manuscript dated 1398

ADDED to the unfamiliarity of names there is the
problem of dates of events occurring over an immense
territory. Even the word 'Muslim' might cause surprise
if people are more used to the older spelling
'Moslem', or many other variants like Mussulman.
'Muslim' is now commonly accepted as the best
rendition of the Arabic sounds in English and will be
used throughout this book.

Readers who know some European history are not

necessarily acquainted with the geography of the Middle-East. What were Ottoman rulers doing in Cairo, for instance, and who were they anyhow, and should one have to worry about Chinese-speaking Moslems in China? Another question, for me at least, is how one reacts to new historical dates so as to make them meaningful using one's own grasp of the history, religion or literature of one's own country. I have some ideas of when the Romans conquered France (easy, about 2000 years ago), and of the death of some of our famous kings, and of course of the 1789 Revolution, and of a few more events nearer the present day with two world wars not so far in the past.

I am an educated person very aware of the enormous gaps in my knowledge. So the best I can do is use my own pegs to situate the rest of the world history as best I can. I cannot remember the exact date of the American Independence, but I know that it preceded the French Revolution by just a few years because Washington was an ambassador at the court in Paris. I cannot even remember the date of a recent world-shattering event like the fall of the Berlin Wall but have a suspicion that it must have been about 10 years ago when I was still living in Cheltenham and so on and so forth. As for the Early Middle Ages, which used to be referred to as the 'Dark Ages', because Western civilization was in decline, the only date to have stuck in my mind thanks to primary school rote learning is 732: Charles Martel stops the Arabs in Poitiers.

So here is a point in common between Old Europe and Islam. It was conflictual history of course, with a battle. Thinking about it now, it dawns on me that presumably there had been many other battles on

French soil before the Arabs reached the centre of France, but I do not know them because the Arabs won! It also seems as if they were an awful long way away from Arab lands and in a rather more glorious phase of their history than the Europeans. So let us go back to the death of the Prophet and trace the rapid expansion of Islam.

The first four Caliphs (632-661)

At this time, Islam had already spread throughout the Arabian peninsula but Muhammad's death without a male heir led to political strife concerning the designation of a successor from among four interest groups. Abu Bakr was elected head of the Islamic community and called 'Caliph', (meaning 'deputy') of the messenger of God. He died two years later but had designated his successor, Umar, who reigned for ten years and conquered large territories, including Syria, Palestine, Egypt, Persia and Iraq. Before his assassination, he also had planned for his succession, and Uthman, from the clan of the Umayya, came to power. He was assassinated fourteen years later because of his unpopular policy of nepotism. Finally, Ali, who was Muhammad's cousin and son-in-law, and believed by some to have been designated originally by Muhammad, was chosen. He was not, however, accepted by the Umayya clan who clung to power and confronted him in battle. Ali was assassinated by one of his disgruntled followers, a member of the egalitarian *Kharijite* sect.

Ali was the last of the 'rightly-guided' caliphs. This is an important landmark in the politico-religious history of Islam since the Umayya party became known as *Sunnis* or partisans of the *Sunna*, 'the practice of the Prophet as related in traditions', whereas the party of Ali or *Shiat Ali* became the *Shia* or *Shiites*. In fact both groups respect the *Sunna* equally, but *Shiites* prefer the traditions which can be traced back to Ali rather than to the other Companions. The chapters on 'Holy text' and 'Sects' explain these concepts further.

The Umayyads (661-750)

After Ali's death the Umayyad governor of Syria claimed the Caliphate and moved its capital to Damascus. When his son succeeded him in 680, the dynasty was effectively founded and twelve more Caliphs succeeded him. It is to be noted that rather than remaining 'Caliphs of the Messenger of God' they became 'Caliphs of God'. Their empire extended eastward as far as the Indus valley and westward to incorporate North Africa and Spain

The Umayyads in Spain (711-1492)

The incursion into Spain is especially fascinating. The Muslims crossed over from North Africa in 711, and Gibraltar, the southern point where they landed, is named after the Umayyad general who led the invasion (*Jabal tariq*=Tariq's mountain). When the Umayyad dynasty established in Damascus fell in 750, one survivor of the massacre escaped to Spain where he ruled as the first of the Spanish Umayyad dynasty. His descendants, styling themselves Caliphs, ruled in Cordoba, (756-1031), and the city became prosperous and culturally advanced. Later on, during their decline, political fragmentation allowed progress to be made by the Christian offensive known as the '*reconquista*' or re-conquering of 'Christian lands'.

Although other Muslim dynasties from North Africa, notably the Berber Almoravids, then Almohads, temporarily regained control, Cordoba was lost in 1236, and Seville in 1248. One small Muslim kingdom remained in Granada, shining with tolerance and civilization until it too fell to Ferdinand and Isabella of Castille in 1492. Now that date is easier to remember as it ties in with another world event of disputed worth to mankind, the crossing of the Atlantic by Christopher Columbus, who 'discovered' America for the Spaniards, who were not slow to export their religion and import the gold, but that is another story.

The Abbasids (750-1258)

Back in the Muslim heartlands, where we mentioned a massacre in 750 (with one descendant saved and escaped to Spain) there was a new dynasty: the Abbasids. There had long been dissatisfaction at the way in which the Prophet's family had been excluded from power and resentment of the luxurious court style which was less brilliant in terms of moral leadership. Although non-Arabs formed the majority of the Muslim community, they were also disgruntled at their lack of opportunities. The Abbasids claimed to be descended from Abbas, the Prophet's uncle, and managed to unite clan, moral and local discontent sufficiently to challenge the centre of power successfully, using forces from Persia.

The victorious Abbasids promptly moved their capital to the newly-founded city of Baghdad. They had of course lost Spain but otherwise the official borders remained about the same. What happened inside was different. The Caliph effectively soon only ruled over Iraq and either received allegiance from

The Taj Mahal at Agra, India, erected in 1635

other 'sultans' (rulers) or not, if other Muslim tendencies established rival dynasties. Even in Baghdad, where other dynasties established themselves, a sort of 'cohabitation' took place by which the caliphate remained linked to the Abbasids.

The Seljuks

The most famous of the sultans were the Turkish Seljuks, who ruled from 1055. Under them the arts and sciences continued to flourish, with great input from Persia, until the abrupt destruction of Baghdad by the Mongol hordes in 1258. The Mongols were pagans and fierce horsemen who had quickly conquered most of Russia, China, Persia and Afghanistan, adding Iraq of course, but also the Caucasus and Anatolia. When their ruler converted to Islam around 1300, Islam had an immense territory over which to expand. But it was the end of the Arab supremacy over Islam, a major departure.

One Abbasid survivor of the Mogul massacre in Baghad escaped and reappeared three years later in Cairo as Caliph in 1261, under the protection of the Mamluk sultan, because it added legitimacy to his rule. This arrangement carried on until 1517 when Cairo was captured by the Ottomans. The Mamluks were in fact Turkish slave guards who had seized power through a palace coup and ruled Egypt and Syria since 1250.

The Ottomans (1281-1924)

As for the Ottomans, whose name may be more familiar, they were originally Turkish tribesmen who, like the Seljuks, were forced to emigrate when the

Mongols were bulldozing their way through. They came against the Byzantine (Eastern Christians) dominions and quickly pushed into Europe and the Balkans, eventually conquering the famous Byzantine capital, Constantinople in 1453. They pronounced the name as Istanbul and it remained their capital until 1922, when the Ottoman sultanate was deposed by the nationalist leader Ataturk who proclaimed the Republic.

When the successful Ottomans took Syria and Egypt from the Mamluks, they brought the last Abbasid Caliph with them to Istanbul where the Caliphate remained until its official abolition in 1924. The sixteenth century had been their golden era when their dominion over the Mediterranean brought them into conflict with Christian kingdoms on many occasions, until the crushing defeat of their fleet at Lepanto in 1571. They were still a threat to Europe in the seventeenth century since they nearly took Vienna in 1683. Incidentally, the delicatessen 'croissant' allegedly commemorates the night when the Vienna bakers, at work while the others were asleep, heard the Turks creeping on the city and gave the alert, allowing the assault to be repelled.

Other Important Dynasties

Many other dynasties ought to be mentioned because of their impact on world politics or culture. The SAFAVIDS in Persia imposed Shiism as state religion and the distinct character of that form of Islam allowed it to resist incorporation into the Ottoman empire and remain within its own borders to this day. The splendour of Isfahan is due to one of its Shahs. The MUGHALS are famous for the decorative style of the miniatures produced by their court artists; they descended from the Mongols and ruled over North India from the sixteenth to nineteenth centuries. Cairo (Arabic *al-qahira* 'the Victorious') boasted the Al-Azhar mosque in 970 which became the oldest university in the world, and rivalled Abbasid Baghdad. Egypt had been conquered by the FATIMID dynasty, which claimed to descend from the Prophet's daughter Fatima and were strongly Shiites. They in turn were conquered by Saladin, the Muslim hero of Kurdish origin who had stood against the Crusaders.

From the time of the Prophet, there had been Muslims in the friendly Christian kingdom of Abyssinia. Traders also carried Islam along their routes so that black Africa and South-East Asia developed Muslim empires, whose expansion was checked partly in the sixteenth century by the colonial activities of European nations.

Decline of Muslim Empires

The eighteenth century saw the decline of all three great Muslim empires, the Ottoman, the Safavid and the Mughal which lost territory and power. There were, however, reformers who preached the revival of a more religious form of Islam, with renewed emphasis on the Quran and Hadith (see Ch.4); a critical attitude to the Muslim rulers of their day for their accommodation with local customs, a rejection of some of the accretions of medieval Islam, and a recognition of the importance of *ijtihad* (the exercise of independent judgement in legal matters).

Within the Ottoman empire, one, Muhammad ibn Abd al Wahhab, opposed Sufism (Ch.9) and popular religion and regarded the Quran and Hadith as the only sources of law; he advocated armed rebellion against the Ottomans and associated himself with Ibn Saud, the head of a minor dynasty in central Arabia. From then on, the influence of the Wahhabis started spreading in Arabia and culminating in their taking Mecca in 1803 and Medina in 1805, where they destroyed all sacred tombs, massacred the local inhabitants and imposed their ways on pilgrims.

European Aggression

European aggression marks the next period, starting with Napoleon's expedition to Egypt in 1798. It reaches its greatest extent when in 1920 the League of Nations (forerunner of the United Nations) gives France and Britain mandates over the newly-created Arab states. Napoleon's occupation is of great significance, not just because it started Egyptomania in France, but more seriously because it was the first time since the Crusades that a European power gained control in the Muslim heartland. The power struggle after his departure and the subsequent history of Egypt leading to dominion by a British Consul General who wielded all the power, will not be told in detail. 1922 marks the beginning of the end of colonization as Egypt is first to be recognized as an independent country, although it does not achieve this status in reality until the Revolution and the evacuation of the Suez Canal zone in 1954. Thus, for a long period of over a century, whether the Dutch in Indonesia or the French in North Africa or the Russians in central Asia, or the British in India and Africa, Europeans colonized most of the lands of the former Muslim empires.

The early nineteenth-century Wahhabis' puritanical power-bid was stopped by the Europeanized armies of the Ottoman Sultan of Egypt, but their religious influence continued to grow and their call to armed action in the cause of religion (*jihad*) did not lose its appeal. About a century later, in 1914, the Sharif of Mecca agreed with the British that he would lead an insurrection against the Ottoman rulers who had allied themselves with Germany, in return for the independence of Arab lands once victory was won; the British, however, signed other agreements (Sykes-Picot 1916, Balfour Declaration 1917) contradicting their promises to their Arab allies, and leading to British and French protectorates in the area and eventually to the creation of the state of Israel.

A New Arab Identity

During that period, prolonged exposure to Western technological influence and growing familiarity with European educational values led to a painful rethinking of Arab/Muslim identity. Different answers were tried in different countries of the Middle East. The exception remained Arabia where an independent process evolved, without references to the West but rather to the Wahhabi brand of Islam mentioned earlier. Abd al-Aziz Ibn Saud (1880-1953) rebuilt Saudi power using groups of puritanical bedouin who were totally committed to enforcing primitive Islam. When they became intractable even to their ruler, refusing to accept the twentieth century on their territory, they were exterminated in battle in 1928. The Kingdom of Saudi Arabia was proclaimed in 1932 and oil discovered in 1938. Power had returned to the cradle of Islam.

Turkey and Iran were not conquered but influenced by Europe and in 1923 the Republic of Turkey was born from the former Ottoman empire and the Caliphate was abolished. The list of countries which obtained their independence between 1922, (Egypt), and 1962, (Algeria) is too long to mention here, or the way in which that independence was gained. After the initial period when nationalist leaders, some Muslim only in name, were supported by their people and carried out some sweeping reforms, disillusion set in with unemployment and unimproving conditions of life remaining the lot of the majority. This led people to see a return to Islam as their only hope.

The anti-Western feelings which often accompanied this Islamic revival must be understood taking into account the artificial borders imposed on Muslim territories in 1920 by Western cartographers and armies. The creation of the State of Israel (1948) and the failure of the United Nations to make it abide by the UN's own resolutions, whilst sanctioning military retaliation in other cases of non-observance, notably over Iraq and Kuwait, remains a cause of complaint. The West's continued interference in sensitive areas it does not understand can also be blamed for the rise of extremist regimes in places like Iran and Afghanistan. Peace and understanding are not yet in sight at the end of our century. Muslim history, as part of world history, is in the making.

Readers will be aware of how difficult it is to select information from such a long historical span covering nearly thirteen centuries and such rich, diverse cultures. Some events have been chosen because it is hoped that they 'ring a bell' for English-language readers whose basic awareness comes from a Western education, Anglo-American media and/or contacts with Muslims.

The monumental legacy of Islamic history surrounds us all, especially in the most resplendent forms of the Taj Mahal or the Isfahan mosques, but also in the humblest converted terrace houses in inner city Britain, although these are now less used as purpose-built mosques begin to grace and renew a post-industrial skyline.

3 Islamic Architecture

Court of the Great Mosque of Damascus, 715

BEFORE attempting to go into the developments of the forms and functions of the types of buildings usually associated with this architecture, so aptly explained by Professor R. Hillenbrand in his latest book, it is perhaps not a bad idea to try and remember what comes to mind if one is not a specialist. Although one might first picture gleaming cupolas and minarets silhouetted on the horizon, other things come to mind, such as patterns and colours, probably coming from tiles covering whole buildings inside and outside. This is clearly not what one would first mention about Canterbury Cathedral or Notre-Dame or the great basilicas of Italy.

It has been said that if you are presented with an untitled photograph of part of an Islamic artwork, you know that it is Islamic but you cannot tell whether it is horizontal or vertical nor whether it comes from part of a ceiling, wall, manuscript, or metalwork, which again would not be said of Western art. This interchangeability of motifs, characterized by calligraphy, geometry, and foliation, combines to create an all-encompassing world. It also points to the interchangeability of functions of different buildings.

Muslims were forbidden to reproduce figures for fear that they would be drawn back to worshipping idols, so that certain forms of architectural adornment like statuary are impossible and do not exist in the world of Islam. Instead, Muslims have mastered the art of reflecting and refracting the light in such a way as to create volume. Stained-glass windows depicting Bible stories are not permitted either; fine lettering which climbs the walls at all angles requests you to apply your heart and mind to the deciphering of the message, in as effective a way. Everywhere, open-ended, repetitive geometrical patterns guide you to the vaults and beyond. The optical effects you experience beat the Impressionists' attempts at rendering the creation of form through colour in changing light.

Traditions of Mobility

As Muslims had a long tradition of mobility, with tents folded for more journeying, carpets and hangings were their most precious possessions. The walls of their permanent religious buildings, which have been compared to tents, are clad with the echo of their prayer carpets.

Muhammad's 'Mosque'

In the beginning, Muhammad is recorded as saying: 'Wherever you pray, that place is a mosque.' It is true that all that is needed for prayer is the *qibla* or correct orientation facing towards Mecca. When Muhammad built his 'house' in Medina, it consisted of a large enclosed courtyard with rooms for his private dwelling tagged onto the outside of one of the walls. All accounts agree that he always led a modest style of life, so the size of the overall enclosure (56m x 56m) points to his thinking of the building more as a community centre than an opulent private dwelling. There, he conducted the prayers for hundreds and when the change of *qibla* was revealed, the palm tree lean-to gallery which served to protect the worshippers from the sun was duly moved to another wall. This first pattern was bound to influence the buildings which followed because of its holy associations.

Although no mosque has survived from the seventh century in its original state, we know of enclosures, sometimes just drawn with ashes or reeds where whole garrisons could assemble at the appointed times (Ch.5) on their marches, and of enormous buildings in cities which became the control points of the expanding empire.

Characterisitcs of Islamic Sacred Buildings

The simplicity of the liturgical requirements characterizes Islamic sacred buildings: an enclosed, orientated space, where hundreds and thousands can fit in for communal prayer which involves ritual movements requiring a space of about 1x2 metres per person. In order for these gestures to be carried out in an orderly fashion by such multitudes, it is advisable that everyone should be able to see the leader of the prayers, the *imam*. It therefore became convenient to have the worshippers in long lines parallel to the *qibla*. This proved decisive in moulding the shape of the future mosques.

The width of the edifice is striking compared with a Christian church for instance, where the cross shape means that quite a few seats in a long nave or transepts would have to be sold 'with restricted view' if it were a theatre. Unlike European Christian architecture which had centuries in which to develop its own forms so that it produced great diversity around the circumscribed area of the Mediterranean Roman empire and in northern Europe, Islamic architecture had to establish itself very fast.

As the Muslims swept from Arabia to Spain and China, they found countries with established civilizations and had to contend with religious buildings as diverse as Byzantine basilicas, Persian fire sanctuaries, or Indian temples. Speed mattered as masses of worshippers had to be accommodated immediately since the new faith required the attendance of all free males, at least on Fridays. Paradoxically, the result is one of unity and buildings soon appeared which established a pattern for Islamic architecture over the vast Muslim empire. In the beginning, the option might have been simply to take over the sanctuaries of conquered people and make them into mosques.

This was done in many places, with the great mosque of Damascus an interesting example, since it was the Christian church of St John the Baptist which itself had used and remodelled the pagan temple of Jupiter. Now, the whole basilica came to be integrated within the mosque by opening it sideways towards the added courtyard. Even there, the influence of the original geographical domain where Islam originated asserts itself, since the mosque is experienced as an oasis with its ablution fountain in the middle of the vast expanse of the sunny courtyard and its covered sanctuary providing welcoming repose to body and soul, its refreshing properties further emphasized by the mosaics of trees and streams in green and blue tones. A Medina in stone?

Two Types of Mosque: *masjid* & *jami*

In general, however, elements from the design of previous buildings were rethought and used for different purposes in custom-designed mosques which were mushrooming all over the Middle East and further. A distinction must be made between two types of mosque, the *masjid* and the *jami* which came to be distinguished within a century of the Prophet's death. The former term, which originates from the Arabic root 'to prostrate', occurs in the Quran. *Masjids* were usually simple affairs everywhere but you might of course have come across splendid ones if embellished by rich patrons. Palermo, the capital of Sicily is reputed to have had 300 mosques, not one of which has survived.

Jami comes from the root 'to assemble' and refers

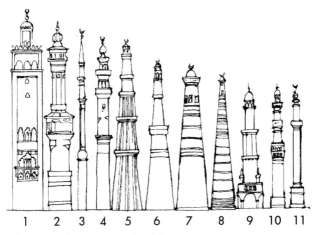

Islamic architecture – the Minaret

Arranged according to scale, **1.** Rabat , Mosque of al-Hassan
(reconstruction). **2.** Mecca, al-Haram. **3.** Cairo, Mosque of
Muhammad 'Ali. **4.** Cairo, mosque and *madrasa* of Sultan
Hasan. **5.** Delhi, Qutb Minar. **6.** Jam. **7.** Khiva, Masjid-i Jami'.
8. Urgench, Masjid-i Jami'. **9.** Lednice, Czech Republic.
10. Hyderabad (Deccan), Char Minar. **11.** Bursa, Great
Mosque. **12.** Samarra, Great Mosque. **13.** Isfahan, Manar-i
Saraban. **14.** Aleppo, Great Mosque. **15.** Bijapur, Jum'a
Masjid. **16.** Mosul, Jami' al-Nuri. **17.** Cairo, Ibn Tulun mosque.
18. Delhi, Jum'a Masjid. **19.** Bursa, Mosque of Murad I.
20. Qairawan, Great Mosque. **21.** Karbala', al-Mashhad al-
Husaini. **22.** Algiers, Jami' al-Sammak. **23.** Agadez mosque,
Niger. **24.** Ghardaya Jami'. **25.** Al-Janad, Yemen.

to the duty mentioned earlier to come to the Friday public prayer. Special permission to build one was required and it conferred the title of town on an urban settlement just as a cathedral confers the title of city on a British town. Grand architectural experiments would take place for their construction. Although the overall plan was as described earlier, innovations took place in *jamis* which show the clever borrowings from other architectural forms and are now part of a typical mosque set-up. Four such innovations stand out: the *mihrab, minbar, maqsura* and dome over the *mihrab*.

Four Architechtural Innovations

The *mihrab* or prayer niche dates from the rebuilding of the Prophet's mosque in Medina in 705 where it might have been incorporated to remember the place where he stood to lead the prayers. The design may have come from churches where the altar was within an arched recess, but it also marked the emperor's throne in antiquity and was therefore appropriate as the caliph, who united political and religious power in the new faith, had the duty to act as *imam* and lead the prayers on Fridays. Elaborate decoration soon adorned the *mihrab*.

The dome over the *mihrab* is the external sign of its pre-eminence. Domes, especially if one remembers the original Pantheon in Rome (or the modern French version) denote greatness, and caliphs were therefore keen to have domes. For inhabitants of crowded cities, a dome which could be seen above the roofs would act as a useful *qibla* pointer.

The *maqsura*, or royal box, obviously requires a ruler and became less frequent as caliphs delegated the role of prayer leader. It served to protect the life of the caliph (two of the 'rightly-guided' ones were assassinated in the mosque and a third one while reading the Quran). It also emphasized, once again, the caliphs' aloofness, as dynasties became accustomed to pomp unknown in Muhammad's times, and also their greatness, so the *maqsura* was situated near the *mihrab*.

The *minbar* is a raised seat at the top of some steps; it can be made of wood, stone or bricks, be movable or not, and is situated to the right of the *mihrab*. The Friday sermon (*khutba*) is pronounced from it. It is similar to a Christian pulpit and bears even more striking similarity to the *ambos* found in Coptic churches, which combined pulpit and lectern functions and were of strikingly close design.

It will be obvious that the *mihrab* is the only one of these innovations found in *masjids*, the others relating more to the princely mosque architecture of the *jamis*. Here you will also have noticed other typical elements: in the courtyard, facilities for *wudu* (compulsory ablution before prayer) and one or many rows of arcades to shield from the sun; inside the covered sanctuary, sometimes a *dikka* (raised platform to allow room for the *imam* not to be pressed by the crowds), and the many lamps with their symbolic meaning of inner illumination, over bare space covered with carpets or matting.

The variations according to dynastic style, local traditions and materials make for an enormous and exciting variety which is difficult to classify but rewarding to visit if you are allowed, depending on countries. In all cases, the sacred character of the enclosure is respected by removing one's shoes,

The Lion Court of the Alhambra Palace, Granada, Spain

which is also a hygienic practice and preserves the carpets from wear and tear.

Manar, the Minaret

The other element which one would be surprised not to find as a component of a mosque is the minaret from which the call to prayer issues five times a day in Muslim countries. It was not always so, because calling from a roof top is equally efficient. Moreover, some puritanical rulers even refused to allow minarets as unwonted refinement not necessary for prayer. Manar, the most usual Arabic term for a minaret means a lighthouse or beacon, or a post or watch tower used to delimit territory. Here again, conjectures abound concerning the Umayyad bid for supremacy in highly civilized Christian Damascus whose inhabitants had to be impressed by tall towers as good as their church bell towers. Whatever its origins and original significance, the popularity of the minaret grew together with experimentations by architects. They used this feature to articulate the mosque's space in various ways, thus giving visible expression – to Muslims of the claims of their faith (tower of strength, light) and – to the rest of the city, of the proud assertion of the existence of Islam. The minaret's incredibly varied designs reflect local enterprise, skills and style and are a delight to eyes and mind.

Other Key Architectural Elements

After concentrating on the mosque, since it is the key to the practice of Islam, we now have to describe other buildings which cannot be understood unless they are situated within the context of Islamic culture. The scope of this book unfortunately prevents us from studying the *madrasa*, *mausoleum*, *caravanserai* and *palace* with all the attention that they deserve.

The *mausoleum* is the only building not to have a respectable origin in the eyes of some Muslims; erecting monuments (especially splendid affairs as several became) as tombs over the graves of dead people was specifically forbidden since the dead believers are supposed to go back to the unmarked earth and all be level with it to emphasize their equality in life and death. The many Arabic terms which depict a mausoleum seem to reflect the unease about each project which was often one of pride and pomp, but was clothed in worthy religious terminology to justify its existence: 'memory to martyrs'; 'threshold to', or 'garden of, paradise'. Making it part of a joint foundation with mosque or *madrasa* helped the founder to have his project accepted, (but in the nineteenth century the puritanical Wahhabis destroyed such structures on their territory).

Adding a canopy above a tomb was supposed to express the shade of paradise above a holy man and therefore canopied-roof structures were permitted, and so on. Popular religion seemed to have favoured association with the holy dead, especially local ones and to be buried at their feet brought the most blessings (*baraka*). It is common in Persia, where groups of mausoleums are the focal points for religious fervour, with visiting of graves for prayers and specific blessings taking place on anniversary or other special days. It also became a way of showing the strength of support for the Shiite imams in Persia when the country was divided between Sunnis and Shiites. Despite many variations, traditional fidelity to the design of a dome on a square structure for mausoleums means that they are more unified in style over the Islamic world than mosques.

The *caravanserai* (or *khan*) is the largest Islamic structure and its prime function was the safe housing of caravans. A single entrance, barricaded at night, led to a square or rectangular courtyard surrounded by a raised platform with arcades leading to chambers for the merchants, unless these were used for the goods if there was a first floor to house the travellers. The animals would be hobbled in the courtyard. There were clearly great differences between the defensive uses of a caravanserai in the countryside and mercantile requirements in the settled, crammed towns. Some were more like self-contained palaces of the desert, used by sultans with itinerant courts. Some may also have been used by the state express couriers who could expect a ready change of horses. Other measures helped travellers on their way to business or pilgrimage: signposts for marshy/foggy/snowy lands, and cisterns and even several routes to avoid traffic jams on the way to Mecca.

Islamic Palaces

Palaces had no religious justification and were not expected to last, but simply to express the new ruler's taste. The result was that although they were finely decorated, few were properly built, and too few have survived. Where they still stand, like the Alhambra in Andalusia or the Topkapi in Istambul, they show that extensive rebuilding commonly took place. They were essentially to be independent complexes with mosque, bath, even cemetery, and accommodation for the ruler's family and retinue as well as barracks, and public and private audience chambers.

Some smaller structures might have been an intentionally idyllic evocation of paradise with beautiful gardens surrounding buildings mimicking what the pavilions of the blessed were expected to be in the next world. In between these two extremes, many other types were also built. All had expanses of water, and some exotic marvel or other to show. Baghdad offered an extreme case of the palace, with the ruler isolated in splendour at its centre, claiming to be the navel of the earth. It was situated in the *qibla* position and its huge territory at the centre of the city only allocated restricted space to the inhabitants who were parked in walled districts in concentric circles.

The *Madrasa* – the Most Islamic Structure

The *madrasa* is the most definitely Islamic structure of all. As it did not originate until the tenth century, there were plenty of Islamic buildings and styles which could be used rather than having to depend on pre-Islamic architectural vocabulary. The institution itself grew out of specific Islamic requirements becoming apparent in the community.

Basically, a *madrasa* is a residential college of higher education which teaches Islamic sciences. These had first been passed on through dictation but by then also involved commentaries and disputations. One of the earliest surviving *madrasas*, in Samarqand, shows that official patrons, princes, teachers or rich families, endowed such buildings and teaching. They tended to be situated in major cities, and be on a large scale to accommodate students from the surrounding province.

One theory is that the steady building of many *madrasas* all over the Seljuk empire, ruled from Baghdad and extending over Iran, Anatolia and into Syria, can be explained by the desire to counteract the teaching of *Al-Ahzar* in Cairo. The Seljuks were ardent orthodox Sunnis whereas the Egyptian Fatimids were Shiites. The Shiites in turn, built more of their own *madrasas* to pursue the ideological war.

The plan of a *madrasa* was based on four *iwans* (vaulted or flat-roofed halls) with their fourth wall opened onto a courtyard. The attractive idea that each hall was used by one teacher, each explaining one of the four schools of law (*madhhabs*) does not hold for Fatimid Egypt but is supported by the evidence of the grandest *madrasa* of all, in Baghdad, which was finished in 1233. Needless to say, that cruciform pattern underwent various local developments and in places would not be recognizable. Many *madrasas* had a mausoleum incorporated for reasons explained earlier. Where space was at a premium, architects placed the students' cells on one or several storeys rather then behind the *iwans*. The rise and fall of patrons, and of the relative status of different provinces, as well as the special interest attached to entrances or domes or other features also explains the richness of the legacy.

The prophet Muhammad would not know his humble dwelling/mosque under the giant gilded marble structure which has replaced it in Medina for the millions of contemporary pilgrims. Worshippers from all over the world and non-Muslims who have seen replicas immediately know that it is a mosque for the Islamic faith.

Great Mosque & minaret, Samarra, begun by al-Mutawakkil in 847

4 Holy Texts: The Quran & Hadith

Texts abound in Islamic art in preference to visual representation

THE QURAN is the sacred text of Muslims. To say that is to say more than what is claimed for the Bible by Christians, since for them Jesus Christ is also the divine Word, whilst for Muslims, Muhammad is the Prophet of God. Muhammad insisted that the Quran was the Word of God which had existed in God's presence from all eternity as 'the mother of the book'. The message he received orally between about 610 and his death in 632 is the text which has been used by all Muslims ever since. It was received in Arabic and is transmitted in Arabic, whether a Muslim's mother tongue is Arabic or not. Translations exist in many languages but they are not the sacred text; a look at the different English ones for instance will show the reader the wisdom of that position.

Muslim children are encouraged to learn the Arabic text by heart. What may seem to an outsider a meaningless task, can also be seen as excellent training in memory work, a skill fast disappearing from contemporary education. In the best cases, it is accompanied by a sense of purpose, and achievement is acknowledged within the family and community.

The text of the Quran is extremely puzzling to a non-Muslim, not just because of the translations but also because of the unusual nature of its composition. It is not a story with a beginning, middle and end. The order in which the 114 *suras* are printed does not follow the chronological order in which they were revealed. To translate 'sura' as 'chapter' is a simple but not altogether satisfactory solution as it is a technical word only used to designate the portions of the Quran and is not applied to any other book. As for the names of the *suras*, they do not correspond to the content. This is because of the importance of oral transmission. The name refers to a special word or incident which will trigger the memory as a prompt: 'The cow' is thus famous for not dealing with cows, but community laws. The *Fatiha* opens the Quran but was a late revelation which Muhammad was told to put at the beginning:

Praise be to Allah, the Lord of the Worlds,
The Compassionate, the merciful,
Master of the Day of Judgement,
Only You do we worship, and only You do
we implore for help.
Lead us to the right path,
the path of those You have favoured
Nor those who have incurred Your wrath or
have gone astray.

His first revelation, however, is in *sura 96*:

Read in the name of your Lord,
Who created: He created man from a clot.
Read by your Most Generous Lord
Who taught by the Pen. [. . .]
Prostrate yourself and come closer.

His last one is *sura 5*. Before throwing one's hands up
in despair, it is worth pondering on the equally
strange, albeit different, arrangement of the New
Testament, which has four versions of the life and
teachings of Christ, placed one after the other, or of
the arrangements of the books of the Jewish
scriptures, (the Old Testament for Christians) which
make sense within a worshipping community, but
probably little outside. Once again, the Quran is
meant to function in Arabic in a heard, and recited
way, and the oral codes involved are not the ones
practised and understood by many in the West, in an
age where the book itself (including 'holy scriptures')
is in danger of losing its meaning and appeal, to
image technology.

How the Quran Came into Being

The manner in which the Quran came into being is
fascinating. Muhammad memorized the revelations
which he believed were brought to him from God by
the angel Gabriel. He recited them to his friends and

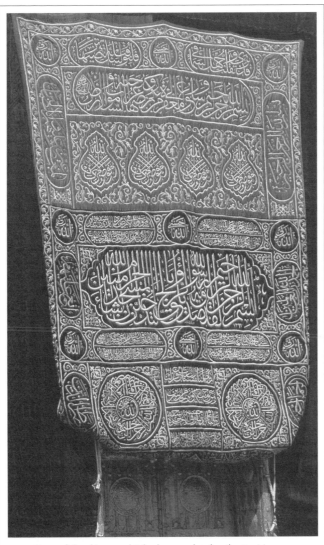

Part of the *kiswa* which drapes the *kaaba* in Mecca

followers who also memorized them and used them in the ritual prayer. After the prophet's death, when many of the men who knew the message by heart were killed in battle, Abu Bakr, (the first caliph) worried about the continued accuracy of the transmission. Umar, (later the second caliph) suggested that Muhammad's secretary and trained reciter (*hafiz*) should write down the text. This single copy was kept by Abu Bakr, who passed it to his successor Umar who entrusted it to his daughter, Hafsa, who had been one of Muhammad's wives.

When disputes started arising among Muslims about the proper way to recite the Quran, the next caliph, Uthman ordered more copies to be made and sent to the different provinces as the only authorized versions. As Uthman's text was not vocalized, several slightly different uses came into being which were rationalized into seven acceptable ways. Later developments, like the fact that the first printed edition was made in Egypt in 1925, using the Kufan system, meant that it became practically the only one available, except in North Africa.

The Quran's Central Message

The central message of the Quran runs equally in the Meccan and Medinan periods: there is only one God, who alone is to be obeyed. There are, however, differences of emphasis between the two phases. The Meccan revelations tend to be shorter, and concern the principles of Islam; they instruct Muhammad to act as messenger, teaching, and comforting him (94):

> Did We not dilate your breast;
> And lift from you your burden;
> Which had weighed down your back?

> Did We not exalt your name? [. . .]
> And unto your Lord, incline.

They expand on God as lord of creation; they attack pagan polytheists who love their treasures more than their social responsibilities (104):

> Woe unto every backbiter and slanderer,
> Who amasses wealth and counts it diligently.
> He thinks that his wealth will make him immortal.

Stories are told about God-fearing people of past ages; paradise and hell are promised to his contemporaries according to their (un)belief and actions in this life. The Medinan *suras* are more elaborate and adapt the message to a growing population of Muslim believers, with many legal precepts aimed at building and establishing the community. They also emphasize God's forgiveness and Muhammad's status, now equalled to that of the prophets, including Jesus, who came before him, to preach God's unity, and call people to repentance and forgiveness. (4,163,170):

> We have revealed to you, as We revealed to Noah and the prophets after him. And We revealed to Abraham, Ismail, Isaac, Jacob, and the Tribes; and to Jesus, Job, Jonah, Aaron and Solomon.[. . .]
> O mankind, the Apostle has come to you with the truth from your Lord.

The wording in both the Meccan and Medinan periods was intended to be understood by Muhammad's contemporaries, with images from the desert and references to their historical situation and practices (81):

> When the sun shall be coiled up;[. . .]
> And the pregnant camels shall be discarded;[. . .]

And when the buried infant shall be asked;
'For what sin was she killed?'

The *suras* also contain much of interest for our contemporary world, often at a loss for values. Some allowances and prescriptions made specific sense in seventh-century Arabia. Whether they still stand as prescriptive nowadays is a question which different schools of Muslim thinkers address differently, much in the same way as Christians and Jewish theologians are divided concerning the interpretation of their scriptures within their religious traditions.

Interpreting the Quran

Interpreting the Quran is an age-old science which has its own rules:
1) the Quran explains the Quran, as unclear passages make sense within the whole context, or a prescription is relaxed or made stricter by a later revelation, because of people's hardness of heart or behaviour.
2) the Sunna explains the Quran on the basis of the *hadiths* (stories, traditions) about what the Prophet had said or done in certain situations.
3) the life-time Companions of the Prophet (including his wives) may be able to throw light on the circumstances of a particular revelation or its meaning.
4) the sayings of the Companions' pupils, the Successors, provided they did not go against one another.

Hadith

The **hadiths** or **Hadith** require special explanation. Because of the difficulty of rendering the Arabic plural, several English ways are acceptable. If one refers to the corpus as a whole, one tends to write 'The Hadith' whereas one tends to refer to specific 'hadiths'. Although the *hadith* have strong authority in the Muslim community, they are not used in ritual prayer, so they do not have the same status as the Quran. Nevertheless, many more attitudes towards what it is right or wrong to do for a Muslim stem from the Hadith than from the Quran itself, which is silent on many points. Many collections appeared after the Prophet's death. It was not just that people loved to remember and meditate on the life of a model leader with an attractive personality: 'the prophetic *hadiths*' have been enjoined in the Quran itself (33,21):

> 'You have had a good example in Allah's Apostle;'

Other traditions also report sayings not incorporated in the Quran but held in great reverence because they were messages from God but put by the Prophet in his own words. A saying of this sort is called a *hadith qudsi*.

Authenticity

An obvious problem concerns the authenticity of the material. Many well-intentioned people repeated what was their own thinking rather than the Prophet's and some acted in a deceitful way for their own benefit, relying on people's gullibility. The Prophet is even supposed to have caught one at it, and how he deflated the liar makes a good story. By the ninth century, there were around 600,000 *hadiths* in circulation! One way of guaranteeing the reliability is to refer to the *isnad* or 'chain of guarantors'. This means checking the names of those who transmitted it orally from generation to generation to assess whether they were reliable.

Two wives, Umm Salama, daughter of Abu Sufyan, and Ayesha, daughter of Abu Bakr, who was learned enough to correct even close Companions, and also authorized the earliest biography of the Prophet, are particularly respected sources of *hadiths*. Different collections are favoured by different Muslim tendencies. The most revered *Sunni* collections were made in the ninth century by Bukhari and Muslim, each including a different number of traditions. The *Shiites* have their own books of *hadiths*. Unlike the charlatans who peddled them for their own profit, the Companions are reported to have been wary of using *hadiths*, lest their human memories should prove not faithful enough.

5 Prayer - *Salat*

Muslim men at prayer

PRAYER, or *salat* is a compulsory duty for Muslims. It is one of the five 'pillars' (*arkan*) or basic religious rituals of Islam. Prayer is meant to establish a rhythmic pattern for believers, so that their day is punctuated by remembrance of God, within the Islamic community. One is reminded of what used to happen in former days within some Christian traditions: Millet's painting of '*L'angelus*' shows French peasants who have interrupted their work in the fields and stand still in order to join in with the praying going on in the village church signalled by the ringing of the bells. Of course, enclosed orders of nuns and monks still observe devotions at fixed times, but they are apart from the community and pray *for* it rather than *with* it.

When Muhammad was at his lowest in Mecca, after the death of his uncle and his wife Khadija, an experience took place which greatly comforted him and persuaded him to continue with his mission. This experience might be described as an 'out-of-the-body' experience in contemporary terms, as his new wife asserted that he never left her side, but many take it to have been bodily. During 'the night journey', *lailat-al-Miraj*, he was transported from Mecca to Jerusalem, and then into the presence of God. As he ascended to the seventh heaven, he discussed matters of prayer with prophets who had preceded him; he then received God's agreement that praying five times a day would be enough. Muhammad had envisaged that fifty times might be necessary!

These prayers were to replace the empty noises made by his pagan contemporaries and were to take place at particular times, punctuating the 24-hour day cycle.

Daily Prayers

Daily Prayers are as follows, as taught by the Hadith:

dawn prayer *fajr* takes place <u>between</u> dawn and sunrise.

midday prayer *zuhr* may be offered <u>between</u> the time when the sun declines from its <u>zenith, and</u> the time when an object's shadow is as long as the object itself.

late afternoon prayer *asr* between that time and <u>just before</u> sunset.

sunset prayer *maghrib* <u>after</u> sunset <u>but before</u> the end of daylight.

night prayer *isha*, preferably <u>before</u> midnight.

The timing of the prayers reveals two elements: the references to the natural order of the cosmos, which has been observed, and is known and used empirically for calculations; also the careful eschewing of the worship of the created order. This is done by cleverly dephazing the worship from the points at which the sun is in its most significant positions, thus reinforcing the notion that it is the Creator who is worshipped.

Because prayer-times depend on the sun, they vary with the seasons. Muslim newspapers and mosques publish local times of prayer, but flexibility is written into the system and approximate times are acceptable. The minaret comes into its own in Muslim countries where the call to prayer is heard at the correct time, and where observance may be enforced in some cases.

The Call to Prayer

The call, *adhan* which was first given from a rooftop by Muhammad's freed slave Bihal, goes like this:

God is very great, God is very great, God is very great, God is very great.
I testify that there is no god but God (twice), **I testify that Muhammad is the Messenger of God** (twice). **Hasten to prayer** (twice). **Hasten to prosperity** (twice). **God is very great** (twice). **There is no God but God.**

When Muslims hear the call, they are supposed to repeat it to themselves, replacing 'hasten to. . .' with 'there is neither power nor strength save in God'. Before the dawn prayer there is the addition: 'Prayer is better than sleep'.

The text in bold refers to the central tenet of Islam. It is called the **shahada** and is the first of the 'pillars' of Islam.

Prayer Is the Second 'Pillar'

None of the prayers needs to take place in the mosque. The Friday midday *salat* which is called *juma* must be prayed in congregation. (62,9):

> O believers, when the call for prayer on the day of Congregation is sounded, then hasten to the mention of Allah and leave off trading.

A mosque is not required; if none is available, any clean place will do, provided that one prays facing Mecca; any object can be placed in front to serve as *qibla* marker. Appropriate, decent clothing must be worn. Ritual purification must be observed, which is why mosques have fountains or rows of taps for *wudu* facilities. *Wudu* consists of washing the hands, mouth, nose, face, forearms, head and feet according to a procedure learnt from childhood. If sexual intercourse, seminal emission, menstruation or childbirth have taken place, then the whole body must be washed. If a Muslim avoids you when you are with a dog, it is because being touched by a ritually unclean animal would mean that he would have to start ablutions again and change his clothes before he could pray.

Performing prayers involves particular recitations and movements. Each co-ordinated unit is called a *raka*. It is obligatory to perform a minimum of two *rakas* for *fajr*, four at *zuhr*, *asr* and *isha* and three at *maghrib*. The *fatiha* which is the first *sura* of the Quran is recited in the standing position. Then follow three or more verses from another *sura*. 'God is very great' is pronounced when changing positions. Bowing from the waist, a Muslim will then say 'Glory be to my Lord the Mighty', and 'Glory be to my Lord the Most High' when prostrating. When sitting at the end of the second *raka*, the worshipper calls blessings on the prophet, makes the testimony of faith and at the very end repeats this, adding:

> O God, send grace and honour on Muhammad and the family of Muhammad as you sent grace and honour on Abraham and the family of Abraham. Surely you are praiseworthy, majestic.

The Friday congregational prayer normally takes place at the mosque for all free males as we saw previously. Women are permitted to attend but are excused if they prefer to pray at home. There is a space reserved for them; this is normally at the back, at the side or on a balcony (to avoid immodest thoughts occuring during mixed prostrations). The *juma* prayer must have a sermon in Arabic before the *rakas*. The sermon (*khutba*) has a set structure: praise of God, a creed, blessings on the prophet, prayers for the Muslim community, a Quranic recitation and exhortation to piety. The *khutba* has always had a political aspect since in the early days of the caliphate, prayers for a particular caliph implied his authority on a particular territory (see *jami* in Ch. 3). If one thinks of a Church of England service with traditional liturgy like Evensong, one could not imagine blessings being called upon any but the ruling monarch during the prayers set for the Royal family.

The call to prayer prefigures the summons on the Day of Resurrection; the ritual purity and cleanliness of the clothes, body and room, represent the call to inner purity. As one faces the *qibla*, one turns away from one's sins in order to turn to God. The bowing and prostrating physically embodies the meaning of the term *Muslim*: one who submits to God in accordance with his will and in harmony with the natural world, or as so beautifully expressed by the Quran:

> 'Those in the heavens and on earth prostrate themselves to Allah willingly or unwillingly, and so do their shadows mornings and evenings'. (13.15)

6 Pilgrimage – *Hajj*

Circumambulating the *kaaba*, Mecca

THE *HAJJ*, or fifth of the five 'pillars' of Islam, is of paramount importance to Muslims, but perhaps the most difficult to understand for non-Muslims. (Pillars 3, almsgiving, and 4, fasting, are explained in the 'Yearly cycle' Ch. 7) After all, throwing stones at pillars, standing for hours in the sun with thousands of others, dressing up in two white sheets, sacrificing an animal, going round a large cubed-shaped building, and spending what might amount to your lifetime's savings in the process, may seem rather alien.

The Pilgrim's Route in Mecca

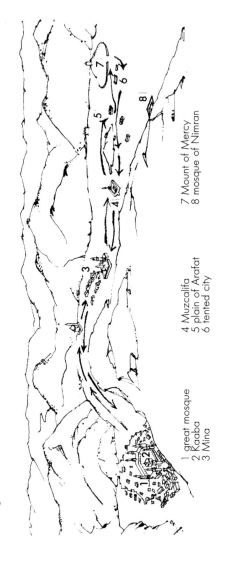

1 great mosque
2 Kaaba
3 Mina

4 Muzdalifa
5 plain of Arafat
6 tented city

7 Mount of Mercy
8 mosque of Nimran

The notion of pilgrimage is not in itself specific to the Muslim faith since it is very much alive in Japan for instance, and was common in former times in Christian Europe. Although it was a commendable undertaking for medieval Christians to journey to places associated with their faith, it was not a duty enjoined on all, nor was it centred on Jerusalem. Rome, the Papal City was favoured, as was Santiago de Compostela in Spain. As for the English, they also went to visit the site of the martyrdom of Archbishop Thomas A Beckett. If we trust the famous *Canterbury Tales*, by Geoffrey Chaucer, written around 1386, we learn that in April:

> Then people long to go on pilgrimages
> And palmers long to seek the stranger strands
> Of far-off saints, hallowed in sundry lands,
> And specially, from every shire's end
> In England, down to Canterbury they wend
> To seek the holy blissful martyr, quick
> To give his help to them when they were sick.

The tales themselves have little to do with pilgrimage; rather, the story-tellers put forward by Chaucer give us an idea of the cross-section of the population which undertook such a pilgrimage. A literary device more than a pilgrim's treatise, his book enshrines a language and a nation in the making and nowadays, both language and pilgrimage set-up are read for their antiquarian and entertainment value, not for their religious content, unless it be cautionary.

If we now go back to the Muslim idea of pilgrimage, and its apparent oddity to non-Muslims, we find that one eminent Muslim writer of the twelfth century, Ghazzali, seems to have thought it odd too, and for him this was precisely the point. To go on pilgrimage is to suspend all normal wordly activities during a few days when pilgrims live solely for God, within the community of believers. It is therefore comprehensible that only Muslims are allowed inside the sacred places where they are going to perform the rites, and that those rites, which nowadays involve between one and two million people from all over the world, should remain as unchanged as possible. They were established by the Prophet and performed by him before his death as a sort of testament and they refer to older stories and events of religious significance (22,27):

> 'And proclaim the pilgrimage to the people. and then they will come on foot or on every lean mount, coming from every deep ravine,
> To witness benefits of theirs, and mention Allah's name during certain numbered days, over such beasts of the flocks as He has provided them with. Eat, then, from them and feed the wretched poor. Then let them complete their self-cleansing and fulfil their vows and circle round the Ancient House.'

The *hajj* takes place between days 8 and 10 of the twelfth month of the Muslim lunar calendar and therefore its dates vary within the Western solar calendar. Strict conditions are enjoined on Muslims who intend to perform the pilgrimage: they must be of sound mind to understand the significance of their journey, and able to accomplish it physically, although there is help with wheelchairs. Financially, the family left behind must not suffer from lack of funds and the pilgrim must have saved the sum necessary for his expenses in an honest way. Because of these conditions, there are let-out clauses which acknowledge that not everyone will be able to perform that duty in his/her lifetime. Muslims who cannot go may send someone else on their behalf, or give their *hajj*

Pilgrims in Mecca

savings to charity. The intention to go, *niyyah* is deemed as worthy.

The other preparation is to place oneself in the state of *ihram* or ritual purity and devout intentions. This includes obtaining the proper clothes: males have to put on two unsewn white cotton sheets, one round the waist, the other over the left shoulder, and leave their head bare. Women wear a plain white garment covering arms and ankles but not their faces (since males around them are expected to have pure hearts). All go bare foot or in open sandals. Equality, self-sacrifice and determination are expressed by these clothes. They are put on while reciting prayers as soon as pilgrims arrive at the entrances to the sacred precinct around Mecca. Many will treasure this outfit and keep it to be buried in.

Once within that area, called the *haram*, no jewellery, perfume or even scented soaps are used. It is forbidden to clip the nails or trim the hair. No animal may be killed, (except those endangering your life like snakes or scorpions). No plant may be cut or damaged. Tempers are to be kept under control no matter how taxing the circumstances. No sexual intercourse or lewdness is allowed (2,196):

> He who determines to perform the pilgrimage during them (the appointed months), shall abstain from intercourse, debauchery and acrimonious quarrel. And whatever you do, Allah knows. Make provision. The best provision, however, is the fear of Allah. So fear Me, people of understanding. [..] So when you take off from Arafat, remember Allah at the sacred monument.

Clear rules govern transgressions. Some offences annul the value of the pilgrimage altogether, others can be redeemed by making amends. Some are excused if accidental.

Day 8 of *hajj*

On day 8, *hajj* proper starts in Mecca. After ablutions, the pilgrims enter the sanctuary where they immediately proceed with the first part of the ritual, at whatever time of day or night they arrive. The anticlockwise perambulation of the Kaaba, performed seven times, whilst calling aloud 'Doubly at your service, O God', and saying other prayers, is the *tawaf*. Pilgrims start at the eastern corner, kissing the Black Stone (or more probably saluting it if they cannot get near enough).

The Black Stone is thought to be a meteorite, which Muslims believe to have been incorporated into the sanctuary structure by Abraham and his son Ishmael as they rebuilt the first sanctuary to the one God, which had been established by the first man, Adam, then abandoned at the time of Noah's flood. The structure became known as the Kaaba, or Abraham's cube and also 'the House of God', *Baitallah* (2,124-5):

> And [remember] when We made the House a place of residence for mankind and a haven: 'Make of Abraham's *maqam* (stand) a place for prayer'. We enjoined Abraham and Ismail: 'Purify My House for those who circle it, for those who retreat there for meditation, and for those who kneel and prostrate themselves;
> And when Abraham said: 'My Lord, make this a city and feed with fruits those of its inhabitants who believe in Allah and the Last Day.'

Around it grew a village, near the miraculous spring of Zamzam, which God had struck to rescue Abraham's second wife Hagar and her son Ishmael when they would otherwise have died of thirst in the desert. The Zamzam well is in the courtyard of the great Mecca mosque. Pilgrims drink its water, and obtain as many bottles of it as they can carry to their relatives and friends back home. When Muhammad captured Mecca, he destroyed the 360 idols inside the Kaaba thereby re-establishing the worship of the one true God. The Kaaba is covered by a black cloth trimmed with gold, the *kiswa*, which is renewed annually because it is cut into pieces and distributed to pilgrims at the end of each *hajj*. It used to be the privilege of the caliph to donate the *kiswa*.

The story of Hagar desperately looking for water and running between the tops of two hills *Safa* and *Marwa* to try and spot any possible help, gives rise to the second ritual, the *sai*: here the pilgrims process at a fast pace (it is called the 'running') seven times between those two places in remembrance of her ordeal and to show their equal dedication to do God's work; it now takes place within an immense corridor (2,157):

Surely, Safa and Marwa are beacons of Allah.

The next rituals involve going to and fro between Mecca and Mount Arafat, about 15 miles away, with every step taken being one of obedience. Arafat is called 'the Mount of Mercy' since it is the place where God forgave Adam and Eve and reunited them with each other. It is the most important part of the pilgrimage and quite arduous to perform. Pilgrims on foot break the journey at Mina whilst others proceed straight to Mount Arafat. The important thing is to arrive there by noon on the ninth day of the pilgrimage.

Day 9 of *hajj*

Day 9 is *wuquf*, the stand on Arafat. This lasts between midday and sunset, in what can be unbearably intense heat. No head covering is allowed for men (since turbans or other types of hats were indicators of rank) but umbrellas are permitted. The long stand is spent meditating on repentance and release from sin, an experience described by pilgrims as exhilarating and unique. Then the two million pilgrims, situated on the Mount or Plain of Arafat listen to a sermon. They next retrace their steps to a camp called Muzdalifa for a night of worship, offering thanks for their release and dedicating themselves for the next day.

At sunrise on day 10, all the pilgrims go back to Mina, for the great day of *Id al-Adha*, the Feast of Sacrifice celebrated by all Muslims, so that pilgrims and those who have stayed behind are associated in religious fervour. It is a very busy day. Pilgrims have to throw pebbles at three stone pillars. This commemorates the place where Abraham, Hagar and Ishmael were tempted by Satan, the Devil, not to obey God and stop journeying to Mount Arafat where the son was to be offered in sacrifice as requested by God to test their faith. Pilgrims show that they too are ready to renounce evil.

The association between the patriarch-prophet and every pilgrim is made tangible by the sacrifice of an animal, chosen according to what each can afford. Afterwards, men have their heads shaved and women cut off about an inch of hair. The pilgrims then go back to Mecca for the farewell circling of the Kaaba. Finally, they return to Mina to recover and celebrate for the next three days.

It may be obvious that even with giving meat to the poor, not all the meat can be eaten. Modern facilities have been introduced in the form of quick freezing and despatching of the meat to Muslim refugee camps. Sometimes, coupons can be bought to the value of an animal which will not be sacrificed there and then but processed later in a *halal* abattoir for the meat to be sent to the needy. The fact that Jeddah airport is the largest in the world does not affect worship as such. The several rebuildings of the Meccan mosque, rendered necessary by the expansion in the numbers of pilgrims, itself made possible by global air travelling, have somehow, provoked unease at the innovation represented by the addition of an extra storey. More worrying still for the Muslim *umma* are the visa restrictions imposed by the Saudi government to limit access, against the religious imperative that all Muslims who can should perform *hajj*.

This in turn touches on the problem of the new political entity of a nation-state, here Saudi Arabia, controlling the place most sacred to all Muslims, and there have been calls for an internationalization of Mecca. The fact that the Saudis are American allies provokes serious resentment. Skirmishes, political or physical, have also occurred with the other oil-giant neighbour of the region, Iran, as both countries are bitter enemies in the doctrinal as well as political fields. The sheer amount of money engaged for the *hajj* affects local economies in very real terms. It is not a simple one-way system, however, as many non-Saudis work in the pilgrimage service industry, as well as in the oil-fields, and are able to plough back their earnings into their home countries, making it possible in turn for more of their fellow citizens to undertake the pilgrimage.

Visit to Medina

As for the pilgrims who have completed the Meccan rites, they are now in a festive mood. If they can, they aim to stay for another ten days in order to visit Medina, 600 kilometres away, where the great mosque contains Muhammad's tomb. Pilgrims greet the Prophet facing his tomb, but no circumambulation is allowed since only the throne of God, represented on earth by the Kaaba, is worthy of such veneration. Other sites in Medina where some of Muhammad's Companions and family are buried are also visited. Grand mausolea had been built to mark them but in their puritanical zeal the Wahhabis destroyed them at the beginning of the nineteenth century; the tomb of the Prophet was later restored.

The *umra* – the Lesser Pilgrimage

As explained earlier, the *hajj* can only take place at a determined time of the Muslim year and involves a gruelling schedule. For those who cannot fulfil its requirements, a form of lesser pilgrimage is possible, which will bring many blessings but will not count as *hajj*. It is called the *umra*, and can be made at any time of the year. The preparation is the same, and the performance of the rituals is the same except that only the first two, the circumambulation of the Kaaba and the seven 'runnings' in the long corridor between Safa and Marwa take place. They are the rituals described as occupying the first day of *hajj* (Day 8) in Mecca only.

It will be obvious that the actions performed during *hajj* only make sense within the symbolic realm of the Islamic religion. However, the yearning to meet God in this life and to stand pardoned in His presence, bringing the hope of being accepted on the Day of Judgement, is an aspiration shared by many .

7 Festivals & Calendar: the Muslim Yearly Cycle

Star & crescent moon – symbols of Islam

ONE OF THE TWO main festivals of the Muslim year *Id al-Adha* has already been mentioned in the context of the *hajj*, or main pilgrimage. We saw it celebrated in Mina, as part of the arduous devotions. It reminds pilgrims of the need to be ready to make any sacrifice for God, which is why, as a token, they have to pay for and sacrifice an animal.

Back home, all over the world, regardless of where they are, Muslims are duty-bound to keep the feast of *Id al-Adha*. This can lead to problems in predominantly non-Muslim countries as there have been cases of horrified neighbours witnessing the slitting of the throat of a sheep on the lawn next door! Reciprocal sensitivity is obviously needed; established Muslim communities do not offend in such a way because abattoir facilities for ritual slaughtering are made available and Muslim practices are no worse than others; some say they are more humane.

Older Westerners may in any case remember the common farm practice of killing one's own animals and preserving them to feed the family through the winter. I am not even sure that it stopped that long ago in France. I also remember the 'Id' sheep penned in a Monoprix supermarket in the Tunisian resort of Hammamet, which one could win with free tombola tickets given with purchases. Our young daughter was more disappointed than her parents at not winning it.

A recent French film directed by a second-generation Muslim immigrant is interesting for its wry portrayal of the mixed identities of the young who remember their Muslim origins because of feasts, yet try to function like the French in order to be integrated: on seeing an Alsatian dog tethered next to his friend's house, a Maghrebi youth jokes: 'Is this your Id sheep?'

What non-Muslims normally notice about the festival is the unusual number of little princes and princesses in the streets as children display their new clothes on visits to friends and families to exchange greetings and presents. There might well be crowds around the mosques too, with people associating themselves in thought and prayer with the lucky ones who are on the *hajj*.

If *Id al-Adha* is the greatest festival of the Muslim year, it seems sensible to try and understand the unfolding of the believer's yearly cycle. Here we come across the tension between the solar and lunar years used to reckon different times. To take an example from a different system, anyone acquainted with the Christian year which determines the Western calendar in varying degree in European countries, will know that Christmas is always on 25 December but that Easter will have to be looked up on the calendar as it may be in March or April; as for Whitsun (Pentecost), people vaguely know that it is some days after Easter (50 in fact). Because of the inconvenience of these moveable feasts for a secular society trying to rationalize holidays and working practices, and because most of them fall on a Sunday when people are usually free to worship anyhow, no special provision is allowed any more. Muslim rituals require more accommodation in the West and schools are now more understanding.

The Muslim Calendar

The Muslim calendar has 354 days and so changes by about 11 days in relation to the 365-day solar Western year. It, too, is divided into 12 months, but they are lunar months, with 29 or 30 days. Each day begins not at midnight but at sunset. As with other religions, festivals help give meaning to the year ahead, because of the echos they carry of all the past practices The word *Id* means 'returning at regular intervals'. Surprisingly few festivals are compulsory in Islam: in fact, only two: **Id al-Adha** already described in the *hajj* chapter and **Id al-Fitr** which concludes *sawm*, the ritual fasting period of **Ramadan**, the fourth great 'pillar' of Islam.

Ramadan

Ramadan is enjoined on all Muslims unless they fall into those categories who are exempt (children under 12, pregnant or nursing mothers, the frail, aged and ill, even travellers on a gruelling journey, not jet-setting). If possible, the non-fasting days must be made up, or food given to the poor instead.

Ramadan celebrates the first revelations to Muhammad. It lasts for a whole month, the ninth of the lunar calendar. Abstinence from food is the most striking element for non-Muslims. It also, however, includes abstinence from sex, smoking and drinking, (even water), during daylight (2,184,186):

> The month of Ramadan is the month in which the Quran was revealed, providing guidance for mankind, with clear verses to guide and to distinguish right from wrong. He who witnesses that month should fast it. But if anyone is sick or on a journey, [he ought to fast] a number of other days. Allah desires ease and does not desire

hardship for you, that you may complete the total number; glorify Allah for his guidance, and that you may be thankful. [. . .] It has been made lawful for you on the night of fasting to approach your wives; they are a raiment for you and you are a raiment for them.[. . .] eat and drink until you can discern the white thread from the black thread of dawn. Then complete the fast till nightfall.

Winter and summer *Ramadans* will entail different deprivations in different countries. The physical discomfort is made bearable by the feeling of community with other Muslims undertaking the same exercise for their faith, as many will go to the mosque to break the fast before returning home to eat. The believers say that they value the opportunity to experience mind over matter, supported by faith. The actual observance of *Ramadan* does not by itself confer spiritual blessings if, once again, the intention is not pure.

The aim of the undertaking is, as in pilgrimage, to take people away from their normal lifestyle and make them re-examine their life in the context of a higher ideal. Experiencing hunger makes you more aware of the poor, and going through real but limited suffering may prepare you for tougher ordeals. This is why families try to be reconciled, to include the excluded and to be generous.

The feeling of community already mentioned is especially apparent when all await to know when the fast is to start; this depends on the sighting of the moon, in the same way as the appearance of the new moon signals the end of the fast and the beginning of the feast of *Id al-Fitr*. The celebrations are similar to *Id al-Adha*, but without a sacrifice. The appropriate greeting for Muslim friends is 'Id Mubarak!', 'Happy festival!'.

The Muslim Cycle of Festivals

It might be helpful to summarize the cycle of festivals during the year, including the dates of other minor days which are not compulsory and depend on local traditions:

MONTH 1: DAY 10; **Ashura**, is an observance rather than a festival, differently approached in various traditions. At first, it had been a time of fasting associated with the Jewish Day of Atonement; when *Ramadan* was instituted instead as the compulsory fast, *Ashura* became an optional fast. It is, however the major day of mourning for the *Shiite* Muslims who grieve for Hussein, the Prophet's grandson who was martyred at the battle of Karbala.

MONTH 3: DAY 12; the Prophet's birthday, **mawlid al-nabi**, was not celebrated before the tenth century, when Muslims probably came into close contact with Christmas celebrations in their Syrian province. The validity of Christmas, a late addition to the Christian year, is disputed by some Protestant Christians. *Mawlid al-nabi*, is much more strongly opposed by the Muslims who find this festival doctrinally unsound whereas at the popular level, many enjoy celebrating it as a renewal of spirituality.

MONTH 7: DAY 27; the night of the Ascent, **lailat al-miraj** when Muhammad was taken from Medina to Jerusalem (where the mosque of Al-Aqsa commemorates his ascent) and to heaven where he was instructed to institute the five daily prayers. The Quran itself does not say any more than (17,1):

> Glory be to him who caused His servant to travel by night from the Sacred Mosque to the Farthest Mosque, whose precincts We have blessed, in order to show him some of Our signs. He is indeed the All-Hearing, the All-Seeing.

MONTH **8**: DAY 15; *lailat al-Barat* the night in the middle of the month which precedes *Ramadan*, when God assigns men's destinies for the next year, is popular with Indian Muslims.

MONTH **9**: DAY 27; the night of power/destiny *lailat al-qadr*: according to the Quran is 'better than 1000 months' and prayers are especially rewarded; (97)

> We have sent it down on the night of Power.
> If only you knew what is the Night of Power.
> The Night of Power is better than a thousand months.
> The angels and the Spirit descend thereon by the leave of their Lord with every command
> It is peace, till the break of dawn.

Although some pious Muslims spend the last ten nights of Ramadan praying through the night because it is not known exactly when the first revelation occurred to Muhammad, the 27th is traditionally celebrated as *lailat al-qadr*; Muslims from South-East Asia try and complete the reciting of the last portion of the Quran on that night. Others normally divide it in thirty portions, one for each day during *Ramadan*.

MONTH **10**: DAY 1; *Id al-Fitr* explained above.

MONTH **12**: DAY 10; *Id al-Adha* explained in the *hajj* chapter.

The overall emphasis of the yearly cycle may be seen to bear on reminding the believers to come closer to God and His Prophet. This is similar to the daily cycle of Quranic recitations which aims at severing Muslims from all too human pursuits. The believers' year is thus one of physical actions (performed or avoided) which, to be valid must be accompanied by devout intentions of rededication of life to the will of God.

The other reminder that individual welfare is in God's hands and is linked to the community's wellbeing is the third 'pillar' of Islam known as 'zakat' or compulsory almsgiving/religious tax. The moving story of the early Medinan converts inviting Muhammad and his band of followers to leave Mecca and dwell among them in Medina also tells how they shared their wordly goods with them. The booty from raids was likewise shared among all the believers, including the new converts. The social cohesion of the *umma*, the community of believers, imposes material solidarity: paying into or receiving cash and foodstuff means belonging to the house of Islam; contributions are also intended to propagate the faith and release slaves and debtors, as well as help the needy and travellers. Ordinary charity is always encouraged, but personal generosity, while it makes for good relationships, does not replace legal alms, as prescribed by the *sharia*.

How 'Giving' is Calculated

A full system was established in classical Islam to regulate the giving, which varied between 2.5 and 20 % of the disposable income. One sheep or goat is to be given per 5 camels owned; 1 sheep/goat per 40; 1 cow per 30; 2.5% of cash, gold or silver; 10% of harvest, but only 5% if the land needs irrigating; 20% of mined produce.

The changed circumstances met in the modern world mean that Muslims have to struggle to decide how to give *zakat* on new commodities, take into account Western tax returns, and practices which are banned in Islam such as interest on credit. Different political systems advocating communal ownership might be attractive to some but *zakat* was intended to be given from individual income.

How much of the administration of the revenue for the good of the community can be done by mosques when an 'Islamic' state exists? Islamic economics exist in an uneasy global context. It is reported that Malaysia saw its income to the Islamic Treasury increase by 70% between 1990 and 1991 as a result of the threat of various punishments to be enforced by the state for evasion of *zakat*.

As with the other 'pillars', however, the intention is paramount if Muslims are to benefit from their actions. The intention indicated by the meaning of the word *zakat* is 'purification'. The portion of wordly goods paid as a religious tax is intended to validate one's possessions provided that they are seen in the context of the ever-valid claims of the needs of the community of God. The yearly giving should be completed by the end of Ramadan.

8 From Cradle to Grave: the Muslim Life-cycle

Mihrab and minbar of the Great Mosque, Tlemcen, Algeria 1082

IN THIS CHAPTER it is hoped to give an idea of what it is like to live as a Muslim. It will be obvious that many different life-styles exist in the world, just as American Christians may not function in the same way as Christians from other continents. They will all, however, have certain festivals in common, and worship on Sundays rather than on other days. As one tries to decide how much they have in common, one may indeed be more aware of the many differences, which in the past have led to religious wars. The many denominations are not our purpose here, not even those in Islam, since the latter will be dealt with in the next chapter. I will therefore concentrate on what makes a Muslim to be considered a Muslim in the eyes of fellow believers.

A new-born baby is welcomed into the world with the words of the *shahada* (profession of faith) whispered in its ear, putting God at the centre of the new life and making it an immediate member of the worshipping community, the *umma*. A piece of date or other sweet food is rubbed on its lips by an honoured aged relative to encourage healthy suckling and to signify that the child is made 'sweet'. Then prayers are recited. The *shahada*, the first of the 'five pillars of Islam', is the simplest to perform as well as the most august to meditate on. In order to be a Muslim, one simply needs to repeat and truly believe the words:

> *Ashadu an la ilaha il-allahu* **(I testify there is no god but God)**
> *Wa Muhammadar rasulullah* **(and Muhammad is the Messenger of God)**.

Muslims utter these words first thing in the morning and last thing at night. These words also form the core of the 'call to prayer', as we have seen in the chapter on prayer.

As for the baby who has thus been greeted and called to be a Muslim, seven days later, it is once more the centre of a ritual as relatives assemble again to choose its name. Muslim names can be quite difficult, because they encompass different categories and are interchangeable at different times. For instance, the parents of a first-born child may become known, no longer by their usual name, but as 'father of X', *Abu* X, or 'mother of X', *Umm* X. The child itself often has a name incorporating the designation *Abd*, 'slave of', followed by one of the attributes of God: the Merciful, the Generous. . ., so Abdullah means 'slave of God'. At this ceremony, the baby's hair is shaved and the same weight in gold or silver is to be given to the poor; if the baby is bald, a generous donation is made too.

Circumcision

Circumcision, or the cutting of the foreskin of the penis, is compulsory. Practices vary as to its timing. It is done at the naming ceremony if the baby is healthy enough. Communities with this tradition find other traditions, especially that of waiting until the boy is between seven and ten, a shameful or cruel practice. Those who are in favour of waiting until that later age encourage the boy with fine clothes, presents and a celebration at which he is the prince. The aftermath has been described in several novels by Muslim writers who had been subjected to the ordeal.

Female circumcision is not a Muslim prescription as is clear from the fact that some African Christians still think it necessary. Egypt being at the centre of the contemporary outrage reflects the strength of a practice going back to ancient Egypt thousands of years before Islam and which has remained part of popular religion. Female circumcision is a much more serious violation of the human person as grave medical and psychological problems are always associated with it. Pandering to ignorant male masses may provide temporary political advantages for courts or governments vying for power but does nothing to enhance the reputation of Islam.

Learning the Quran, Manners & Hygiene

At around the age of four, some Muslim children are asked to learn their first Quranic lesson in Arabic, repeating the *Bismillah* which prefaces every *sura* (except for one). 'In the name of God, the Compassionate, the Merciful'. It therefore makes sense to memorize the words which are going to act as *aides-mémoire* as the learning progresses.

Manners and hygiene are also developed. The importance of the ritual washing before prayers has been dealt with in the chapter on Prayer (5). By contrast, matters of private hygiene are normally personal choices for Christians so much so that they are not even mentioned in religious education. Who was ever told that they had to go to the toilet in a certain way or have a bath after making love, and not come to church with body odours including garlicky breath, or not persist on ringing the bell or knocking more than three times if friends do not answer the door, as they are entitled to privacy? We know too little concerning Jesus' actions to emulate every detail of his life-style; 'following in his footsteps' is more of a figurative guidance. Perhaps the Maunday Thursday ceremony of washing the feet (supposedly of the poor) in church, as Jesus did to teach a lesson of humility, can help us understand the desire of the Muslims to perform every possible human action in imitation of the Prophet, since his ways were the closest to God.

The *hajj* terminal at Jeddah Airport

The *sharia* or 'Path'

The SHARIA OR 'PATH' is often misunderstood in the West as an inflexible set of rules, partly because of the bad publicity given to it by vociferous Islamist groups; in fact it is designed as a two-faceted approach to help even the most vulnerable in society be accepted as a member of a God-fearing community. It aims to provide all guidance in fulfilling the religious duties which qualify you as a Muslim, the famous *arkan* or 'five pillars of Islam' which cannot be performed without attendant purity, ritual and personal. But the *sharia* also covers interpersonal relationships, which also involve ritual purity and personal hygiene, as some of the examples above will have shown.

Islam is not afraid to mention sex as a powerful agent in human lives, which must be taken fully into account but also considered in the light of the higher calling to be submitted to God. The observation, given earlier, about sex during Ramadan is one example. There are reports of men coming to Muhammad worried about whether sex with their pregnant wife might be harmful to her or the baby. Men are advised about pleasing their wives before taking their own pleasure, but not to worry about rules concerning positions. Marriage is enjoined on all. The Prophet said: 'When the servant of God marries, he perfects half his religion'. This means that even members of mystic orders marry rather than undertake vows of celibacy. It also means that homosexuality is not recognized.

Women and Islam

The situation of women in Muslim society is a provocative issue between the West and Islam. The first thing to avoid is essentializing any one aspect or trusting media reports. There is no such person as Muslim Woman; rather many different voices to be respected. It is also helpful to keep a perspective and be aware of one's own country's promotion of female welfare and equality, or otherwise. France had to wait until 1997 to see a significant number of women elected to Parliament, and has never yet had a female President; a wife's property and earnings were the husband's until the 1960s; even now, the 'glass ceiling', or hidden inequality of the sexes when promotion is concerned, remains entrenched in Western societies; advertising glamorizes and debases women as sexy gimmicks for selling cars or other products, whilst girls become anorexic because they cannot accept their own bodies deemed unfashionable on the current market; in such a context, Western society should be wary of casting the first stone at Islam for fear of ricochet. In 1603, Shakespeare could still have Laertes advising his sister Ophelia against too close an intimacy with Hamlet (I, 3,35) thus:

> The chariest maid is prodigal enough,
> If she unmask her beauty to the moon:
> Virtue itself 'scapes not calumnious strokes:

Some aspects of women's legal status in Islam are, however, undeniably not egalitarian. A sister inherits only half the share of a brother, and a male witness is worth two females. A man may unilaterally divorce his wife; she cannot divorce him unless he has failed her in a few recognized ways and she then has to petition a court. A man may marry a non-Muslim; a woman may not unless he converts. Four wives are allowed, but only one husband. Against this, in Christian Europe where the first-born male used to inherit all the estate, with some allowance made to younger sons and dowries provided for females if money was left, the females would have been glad to be entitled to half their brother's share! Muslim jurists explain this inheritance law as fair because when a female marries, she retains all her own property, whereas her husband must by law keep her financially even if she is the richer of the two.

All examples cannot be examined in detail here. Anthropological, sociological, historical, economic and especially political contexts would have to be assessed. Globalization and dislocation affect every country and many rural areas of the globe populated by Muslims are feeling disruptive shocks more strongly than the post-industrial societies in the West. The position of women appears to many people deprived of any stake in their own lives as the one visible asset for guaranteeing a survival of identity. In this way, the West and its officially democratic values may be responsible for the very hardening of the condition of Muslim women.

A feminist Moroccan Muslim sociologist, Fatima Mernissi, explains how all hopes of challenging male bastions disappeared after the bombing of Baghdad during the Gulf War which shattered all Muslims: the debate concerning the wearing of a veil in public could no longer be the prime agenda when Muslim identity had been violated. This of course does not justify the Algerian government's betrayal of women when in 1984 it re-imposed a 'family code' removing the status of adult from women, who thought that the heroic role they had played in the liberation war against France was sufficient proof of their adulthood. It was yet another example where political expediency played a bigger part than Islam in the imposition of 'Islamic' laws, and as usual, to the detriment of women.

Marriage and Islam

And so back to the marriage stage in the Muslim life-cycle. Marriage is not a sacrament but a contract. During this ceremony, a dowry is agreed, which the husband must pay to his future wife, not her father, in two parts: a small one at that stage and the larger share if he divorces her; if she divorces him, she must return the first amount received. A woman does not have to take her husband's name. Cousin marriages which are frequent in some groups, can be a problem because of the inbreeding involved.

Arranged marriages are encouraged in the hope that a careful matching may be more successful than the young romantic love exalted in the West which is followed by such a high rate of divorce. It also reflects the higher status accorded to the community since links created through the marriage bind the extended family in a supportive network. No man or woman, however, should be forced to marry a partner against his or her wishes. Ideally, compatibility is the expected norm, especially that of piety, which should outlast wordly advantages and gives a fairer chance to anyone, even the poor or ugly.

The marriage contract does not need to be made in a mosque or to involve an imam. It does, however, need to be a proper transaction and legally-binding clauses can be inserted by either side: a woman may register that she will not accept a second wife. Readings of the Quran and prayers then take place, as well as an exchange of vows in front of a minimum of two witnesses, God's presence being invoked as the greatest witness. The wedding party is held a few days after husband and wife have lived together. Guests come to share in a festive meal and offer presents, usually of money. Sex is expected to be mutually enjoyed within a stable loving relationship which excludes sex outside marriage. Every child born must have a legal blood father. This explains why adoption is illegal in Islam, despite strong encouragement to foster orphans or children of people in difficulty. No man can take away from the real father his paternity, not even after his death.

Divorce and Islam

Despite every care being taken for the marriage to be a success, Islam recognizes the frailty of human beings in a more generous way than most other religions. Divorce is discouraged, but is not a religious or social stigma. Muhammad offered to divorce any of his wives who did not like her life with him:

> O Prophet, say to your wives: 'if you desire the present life and its finery, so come along that I might provide for you and set you free kindly.
> But if you desire Allah, His apostle and the life to come, surely Allah has prepared for the bene-ficent among you a great wage.

Remarrying is common for divorcees and widows. Mutual consent and amicable settlement is encouraged by the Quran as a lesser evil. In any case, a period of waiting is compulsory to check that the wife is not pregnant, and to allow for reconciliation. After that period, if the couple desire to remarry, it is allowed provided that she has been married and divorced from another partner in the meanwhile (2,229):

> If he divorces her, she shall not be lawful to him again until after she has married another husband.

This is meant to protect the wife from being at the beck and call of an angry husband. By making the divorce final, he must realize that she cannot be his again at his next whim.

The worst case of divorce is if the wife is accused of adultery. Four male witnesses have to prove that this actually took place. Whilst shameful practices have been reported where rape of the innocent woman is then construed as adultery, instances of earlier times point to that measure being instituted rather to make it impossible for a jealous husband to harm his wife with his suspicions (24,4):

> Those who accuse chaste women, then cannot bring four witnesses, whip them eighty lashes, and do not ever accept their testimony. For those are the wicked sinners.

If nothing can be proved and the marriage is irretrievable, they are divorced and left to God's judgement, since He alone knows the truth.

Begetting children is encouraged as they in turn are supposed to honour and look after the needs of elderly parents. Older people are entitled to be treated with more attention than young children and are normally cared for at home. The practice in modern households in the West is, however, evolving, as care for the Muslim aged is becoming a problem similar to that of non-Muslims because of changing life-styles. Muslim homes for the old are appearing in Britain.

Once in a lifetime, a devout Muslim who can perform the pilgrimage to Mecca, is required to do so as part of his or her duty. This involves financial and other planning which naturally has an impact on the family's behaviour before the visit. They may also become more involved in religious practices affecting their daily cycle, with prayers becoming more regular after their visit to Mecca. The yearly observances may then be more devoutly observed. For a description of the actual pilgrimage, see chapter six.

Death and Islam

Death, too, the unavoidable and expected boundary of the life-cycle, is prepared for in the *sharia*. When a person is dying, relatives and friends should assemble. The dying one asks for forgiveness and blessing from them and from God. They encourage the dying person to say or at least hear, the *shahada*, first heard at birth so that God seals his or her lips and ears as He had opened them. The body then receives the last complete ritual washing as soon as possible after death. The corpse is anointed with scents or spices and wrapped in a shroud of three unsewn white sheets for a man, or five for a woman. If the person has been on the *hajj*, then the *ihram* cloths which had been dipped in Zamzam water may be used.

Martyrs are buried with their bloodstains unwashed and preferably where they died. All others should be buried without a coffin, simply carried to the cemetery on a board in their shrouds. No monument should be erected in order to remind the living of their equality in life and levelling in death. Burial is required to take place within twenty-four hours of a person's death.

Mourning should not be excessive in display of grief or last more than a few days, because of the hope of reunion at the resurrection and because the righteous should be pleased to reach happiness quickly even if they leave their loved ones behind, as Muhammad was warned when grieving for the loss of his children. Widows are allowed more mourning time and should wait for about 130 days if they wish to remarry. Some Muslims like to go to the grave forty days after the burial for prayers of remembrance, but others disapprove. The relatives of the deceased are visited often and by many who show their respect for the departed and comfort the bereaved.

In non-Muslim countries, problems can arise with local legislation and customs. A special plot should be available to the Muslim community so that the graves can be dug to allow the dead to be buried with their heads to the right, facing Mecca, and to be guaranteed to hold only one person. Immigrant Muslims who have not felt at home in a European country prefer to be flown back 'home' and be buried in a proper Muslim way. More settled communities have their rights acknowledged.

Muslim Life and the Diaspora

The economic and political diaspora of Muslims in the West is a relatively new phenomenon since decolonization. The combination of ignorance in the new, often uneducated immigrants, and the assumed self-righteousness of the host countries has often made simple requests appear as dramatic bids. Unwholesome rhetoric on both sides has not helped ordinary people live ordinary decent lives.

Some of the religious requirements like mosques, or time and space to pray at work on Friday lunchtimes, or ritually slaughtered (*halal*) meat available for home but also in school (or a vegetarian menu instead), or the possibility for females to make up their own minds about wearing a headscarf or not, without pressure from some and discrimination from others, are issues affecting the relations of Muslims and non-Muslims in a sometimes demanding way. It is the case in France for instance, where Islam has become the second religion in just a few years, at a time of increased political tensions with Muslim countries.

All these factors affect the life-cycle of Muslims, and not only of those who have settled as citizens of non-Muslim countries. Through its network, the wider community of the *umma* is forced to re-examine the tenets of its faith and religious practices in a global environment.

9 Denominations and Sects

Sufi 'whirling dervishes'

ANYONE acquainted with any religion will be aware that not all its adherents agree on its doctrinal basis, the meaning of its scriptures, and the practices required to be a member. Sects exist or have existed from A for Anabaptist to Z for Zealot. Islam is no exception and can boast a range extending from Ahmadis to Zaidis. Although in our century of ecumenism, Orthodox, Catholic and Protestant Christians meet round a conference table more often than on the battlefield, bitter quarrels have envenomed the past.

An impartial observer might be forgiven for doubting the value of any creed which turns human believers into murderers. Alternately, others might admire the strength of conviction which is responsible for martyrs and saints. Very often, the detail over which people die appears trifling, bizarre and at best a matter of opinion beyond proof to anyone not involved. Yet failing to understand the depth of feeling which religion can stir even in the twentieth century, and remaining on the level of sociological analysis misses the point. Historical events are constantly being rewritten in people's lives. Today, in July 1997, newspapers report that the two surviving widows of American soldiers who fought on opposite sides during the Secession/Civil war in 1865 had had a symbolic reconciliation meeting.

The variety within Islam has been mentioned on several occasions, concerning festivals, architecture, schools of law and interpretation, and of course early historical disagreements concerning the Caliphate. The centrality of its 'five pillars', however, provides a steady basis. The first one of these, the *shahada*, is the determining element which can be used to decide whether some beliefs and practices fall within Islam or not, rather than national or other rivalries as is sometimes the case. Divinizing a human being or accepting another prophetic revelation after Muhammad's is the definitive watershed. Thus, one can say for example that the Bahais, the Ahmadis and the members of the Nation of Islam are not Muslims, although the first two grew out of Muslim communities and all three have similarities with Islam. If we start with the most frequently mentioned sects from various parts of the world, arranged in alphabetical order, we find the following short list.

The Main Sects Not Recognized by Islam

The **Ahmadis** are an Indian movement, who tried to incorporate Hindu and Christian symbolism and mix modernist theology and social conservatism with evangelistic zeal. In Pakistan, they are not allowed to call themselves Muslims, and, they are banned from Mecca, because they revere their founder as a prophet.

The **Alawis** of Syria, of which president Asad is a member, deify Ali and believe in the transmigration of souls, which also puts them beyond the pale.

The **Bahais** are another offshoot of Shiism, but they have their own scriptures and regard their prophets as equal to Muhammad, which excludes them. After persecution, large numbers emigrated from Iran to Europe and America where they are active in multifaith encounters.

The **Druzes** are an offshoot of the Ismailis and live mainly in the Lebanon and part of Syria; one of their leaders proclaimed one of the Fatimid caliphs as divine, which puts them outside Islam. The secrets of their religion are closely kept by their elders.

The **Nation of Islam**, known popularly as **Black Muslims**, is an American development, first called 'the lost-found Nation of Islam', started in 1930 among the poorest blacks who were taught that black people descended from a black God, whereas the whites were creations of the devil. Their second leader, Elijah Muhammad, was revered as being the Prophet Muhammad, a heretical view. His second-in-command, Malcolm X, however, changed his views after going on pilgrimage to Mecca and witnessing all races worshipping there. Elijah Muhammad's son, who succeeded him in 1975, reformed the movement along genuine Sunni Islamic beliefs and renamed it '**the American Muslim Mission**'; it is now supported by Arab states. A breakaway group, however, appeared in 1979 under the leadership of Louis Farrakhan, which named itself 'the Nation of Islam' to show that it intended to go back to the doctrines of the original sect.

Early Crises

If we now go back to the first century of Islam and to the first rift within the Muslim community, we notice that it happened soon after the death of Muhammad, and concerned his succession. Several pressure groups were vying for leadership, according to different interpretations of how best to continue building the community after the loss of its unique, charismatic leader. Should the 'best qualified' or a family descendant be selected? What makes a leader, the best? Is it because of proven skills, perhaps acquired as a member of an established powerful group before conversion to Islam? or because of his personal piety, thus making the caliphate available even to a non-Arab slave?

We saw how early decisions were made concerning the first four 'rightly-guided' caliphs and how three out of four were murdered by other Muslims who disagreed with their decisions. We also came across references to the *Shiites'* Day of Mourning on 10 *Muharram*, to their splendid mausolea in Iran and to dissentions concerning the pilgrimage to Mecca, under Saudi control. The *Shiites* are an important part of the Muslim family, representing about 10 % of its members, whereas 90% are *Sunnis*, or mainstream Muslims, who despite different geographical and cultural backgrounds, believe and observe the *sunna*, the path of tradition relying on the Quran and the community for guidance in the continued interpretation and practice of Islam.

Although the *Shiites* are now a minority, there have been times in history when the balance of power seemed to favour them, especially in the tenth and eleven centuries when the *Shiite* Fatimid dynasty controlled Egypt, Syria, and Palestine, and were the guardians of Mecca and Medina. At the same time, Iran and Iraq were ruled by another *Shiite* dynasty. Then came the *Sunni Seljuks* who subdued all these territories and re-established *sunni* practices and beliefs, using the *madrasas* mentioned in the chapter on architecture (3).

The Shiites

The word *Shiite* comes from *Shiat Ali* and means Party of Ali. As a group, they are called 'the Shia' or as a collection of individuals, the Shiites. Ali, as we saw earlier was Muhammad's cousin and son-in-law, a pious man, early supporter of Muhammad, and brave warrior termed 'Lion of God'. He was bypassed three times before becoming caliph and some held that he was the only true caliph, the first one. Of his two sons, Hasan relinquished his claim to the caliphate for a life of piety, but Hussein challenged the rival dynasty settling in Damascus, under the tyrannical Yazid.

The battle of Karbala (680) saw Hussein and many of his family, even babes in arms, killed pitilessly. After that, the Shiites became passionately attached to the family of the Prophet and its remnant, exalting martyrdom with peculiar devotion, some would say fanaticism. The strength of the Shiites' feelings can be judged by the fact that in 1979 the regime of the

Shah of Iran could be toppled by clerics. They were following Khomeini's lead to present the struggle as a reenactment of the battle between the hero Hussein and the Damascus villain of old, Yazid.

The sometimes gruesome yearly passion-play performed in the streets commemorating Hussein's martyrdom expresses the cruelty of his death for the community, and keeps historical memories alive. Devotion is also obvious at the shrines of Ali's grave, the site of Karbala, and Meshed in Iran, a centre of learning around the tomb of Imam Rida. These even supersede Mecca in popular piety and have been used as alternatives for *hajj*.

Imams – 'Imbued with the Light of Muhammad'

Shiites can be seen to insist on the charismatic aspect of the figure of Muhammad as the link between human beings and God and they imbue his family with similar qualities, to guide the believers. These privileged people are the Imams (a term not to be equated with the usual meaning of 'prayer leader' in a mosque). They are endowed with mystic qualities, as the sole interpreters of the inner meaning of the message, since they are imbued with the original 'light of Muhammad'. This does not prevent them from being scholars and in fact they have preserved the rationalist theological tradition dating back to the eighth century.

Shiites are divided as to the number and lineage of the Imams, the main branch acknowledging twelve, hence their name of 'Twelver Shiites'. From the tenth century, the last Imam withdrew from the world; he is now concealed, but still in control and will come back as the *mahdi* before the Day of Judgement.

Ismaili Shiites

These differ from the above about the line of succession after the death of the sixth Imam in 765. He had two sons, Ismail and Musa. The elder, Ismail, died before his father who therefore nominated Musa as his successor, say the Shiites. Not so say the Ismailis; Ismail was hidden by his father for safety, and was succeeded in turn by his son Muhammad, who then went into occultation, but will come back as the *Mahdi*. This at least was the early doctrine.

Today, however, their current leader is Agha Khan IV, revered as 49th Imam. How they came to this view is very complex. At some point the Ismailis split into more groups, one of which believed that their leader was the next Imam (instead of waiting for the return of the hidden one). At their zenith, under the name of **Fatimids**, we have seen them ruling Egypt and North Africa in the tenth century. One sub-group is known in English as the '**Assassins**' from their nickname *Hashishiyyin* 'hashish eaters'; they are famous for their eagle-nest of Alamut from where they sent assassination squads against political opponents. It must be noted, however, that there is no evidence that they were hashish users, or that their methods of settling disputes were any different from their adversaries'.

Even the 'Assassins', however, could not hold against the Mongol hordes. The Ismailis reappeared on the Muslim stage in the nineteenth century when the Shah of Persia granted their Imam the title of Agha Khan, 'prince'. He later established his base in Bombay, where most members lived. They have a cyclical view of history; with every seventh Imam abrogating the previous *sharia* and enunciating the next. They still suffer from being considered inferior by the Sunni majority, although they are well-known internationally through the many charitable educational foundations the Aga Khan endows from his wealth.

Sufism

Although Sunni and Shiite Muslims may seem very divided to an outsider or to many of their own members, there are similarities in the devotional field where Sunni *Sufism* is alive. **Sufism** probably takes its name from its first exponents who were ascetics wearing coarse wool (*suf*) garments, as a reaction against courtly pomp. Later, they may have reacted against a rationalistic philosophical approach to religion, preferring to emphasize God's love. A famous woman mystic, Rabia of Basra (d. 801) has left us this prayer:

> O God, if I worship Thee in fear of hell, burn me in hell;
> If I worship Thee in the hope of paradise, exclude me from paradise;
> But if I worship Thee for Thine own sake, withold not Thy everlasting beauty.

Sufis then developed the doctrine of losing consciousness to become absorbed into God. While extreme practices gave Sufism a bad name at times, it is concerned with leading people to God through various stages on a path of enlightenment. There are different *Sufi* orders, each with its elder (*shaikh*) and disciples, often part of an international network, with its own discipline and ritual, including the recitation of set mantra-like prayers.

The 'whirling dervishes' go back to the Persian poet Rumi (d.1273). One famous mystic, a thirteenth-century Spaniard named Ibn al-Arabi, made it easier for Islam to spread to south-east Asia because of his understanding of the presence of God in everything. He was a Sunni but had many Shiite followers. This is not surprising as the *Sufis* believe that there is a saint or 'friend' of God who is present in every age as the 'axis', at the top of a spiritual hierarchy often traced back to Ali. This leader throws light on the inner meaning of the Quran and Hadith.

Such an idea is therefore quite close to the Shiites' doctrine of the succession of infallible Imams. *Sufism* seems to appeal anew, often at the popular level, to young Muslims growing up in secular Western countries, and therefore anxious to acquire an identity through distinctive Islamic practices.

The variety present in Islam can be read as bewildering or as a testimony to its rich and enduring appeal as a religious system embracing body as well as soul, the personal as well as the political. It is full of paradoxes. The majority of people in Islamic countries are illiterate and yet they show immense reverence and pride in 'the Book' and in some of the most exquisite calligraphy in the world. There are female Muslim prime ministers and mystics, but many women still walk Islamic and Western streets veiled in black from head to toe. Islam dominated the fields of philosophy, medicine and the arts when Europe was still in the 'Dark Ages' and yet it is principally because of the recent discovery of oil and the resulting financial power that this gives, that it now counts on the world scene once more. Islam lays down many rules but allows for even more exceptions to those rules, and it has produced great cultural diversity from a remarkably simple confession of faith, which all are invited to make but to which none is compelled:

> 'I testify that there is no god but God and that Muhammad is his Messenger.'

The Five Pillars of Islam or *arkan*

The Creed or *SHAHADA*

The Daily Prayers or *SALAT*

The Compulsory Almsgiving or *ZAKAT*

The Ritual Fast or *SAWM*

The Pilgrimage or *HAJJ*

The Dome of the Rock, Jerusalem. Built by Abd al-Malik in 691

Glossary

English spelling has been used throughout to convey the nearest pronunciation to the Arabic sounds. All diacritic marks have been removed, even standard ones, like ' in Qur'an, for ease of reading.

adhan   call to prayer
arkan   pillar
bismillah   the opening of the invocation 'in the name of God'
caravansarai or *khan* lodging place for travellers
dhikr   repetition of pious formulae, used in Sufi practices
fiqh   science of religious law
hadith   traditions about Muhammad's sayings and actions used for guidance in all aspects of life
hajj   pilgrimage to Mecca during the twelfth month of the Islamic calendar
hijra   beginning of the Islamic calendar commemorating Muhammad's emigration from Mecca to Medina
id   festival
ijtihad   use of independent reasoning instead of repetition of past judgement
imam   for the Sunnis leader of the prayers in a mosque; for the Shia, infallible guide to the inner meaning of Quran and Hadith
jahiliyya   state of pagan ignorance in Arabia before Islam
jami   Friday mosque

jihad	holy war
kaaba	the House of God on earth; sacred sanctuary in Mecca containing the Black Stone, to be circumambulated during pilgrimage
kiswa	covering of the Kaaba
khutba	Friday sermon
madhab	school of Islamic law
medina	city
maqsura	royal box in the Friday mosque
marabut	local saint or his/her tomb
masjid	simple mosque
mihrab	arch or niche in a mosque indicating the direction of Mecca
minbar	pulpit in Friday mosques
miraj	Ascension of Muhammad to heaven
muezzin	man calling to prayer
muqarnas	honeycomb type of design in vaulting
qibla	direction of prayer (Mecca)
quraysh	main tribe in Mecca, of which Muhammad was a member, but which opposed him
Quran	God's revelation to Muhammad
raka	a unit of prayer including words and postures
ramadan	month of fasting
sai	the 'running' between Safa and Marwa as part of the pilgrimage ritual
salat	ritual prayer, practised 5 times a day
sawm	fasting
shahada	profession of faith
shaik	leader (tribal chief or religious elder)
sharia	the divine law,
shia, shiite	a Muslim denomination especially attached to Ali
sunna	customary practice of Muhammad

sunni	adherent of the Sunna, usually meaning the mainstream Muslims as opposed to the minority Shia (although they also follow the Sunna)
sura	a portion of the Quran
tafsir	Quranic commentary
tariqa	Sufi brotherhood
ulama	Islamic scholars
umma	the community of believers extending beyond political or geographical borders
umra	the lesser pilgrimage to Mecca, possible at any time of the year
wudu	ritual cleansing of the body before religious observances
wuquf	the 'standing' near the Mount of Arafat, as part of the pilgrimage ritual
zakat	compulsory almsgiving

Further Reading

The Qur'an, a modern English version, translated by Majid Fakhry, Garnet Publishing company, Reading, 1997

K. Cragg and R. Marston Speight, *The House of Islam*, Wadsworth Publishing Company, Belmont, California, 1988

R. Hillenbrand, *Islamic Architecture, Form, function and meaning*, Edinburgh University Press, Edinburgh 1994

P.M. Holt, Ann K.S. Lambton and Bernard Lewis, eds. *Cambridge History of Islam*, Cambridge University Press, 1970

I. R. Netton, *A Popular dictionary of Islam*, Curzon Press, London, 1992

N. Robinson, *Islam, The Sayings of Muhammad*, Duckworth, London, 1991 forthcoming 1998

W. Montgomery Watt, *Muhammad, Prophet and Statesman*, Oxford University Press 1961

A. Rippin, Muslims, *Their Religious Beliefs and Practices, Volume 2: The Contemporary Period*, Routledge, London 1993

Index